Living by Faith

DAVID VENABLE
Living by Faith
Weekly Devotions

Outskirts Press, Inc.
Denver, Colorado

I wish to dedicate this book to all my grandchildren, those already born and those not yet born. May they all take the concepts in this book as the floor of their experience in Christ and move to even higher places.

The opinions expressed in this manuscript are solely the opinions of the author and do not represent the opinions or thoughts of the publisher. The author has represented and warranted full ownership and/or legal right to publish all the materials in this book.

Living by Faith
Weekly Devotions
All Rights Reserved.
Copyright © 2011 David Venable
v2.0

Unless otherwise noted, Scripture quotations are from THE HOLY BIBLE, NEW INTERNATIONAL VERSION®, NIV® Copyright © 1973, 1978, 1984, 2011 by Biblica, Inc.™ Used by permission. All rights reserved worldwide.

Cover Photo © 2011 JupiterImages Corporation. All rights reserved - used with permission.

This book may not be reproduced, transmitted, or stored in whole or in part by any means, including graphic, electronic, or mechanical without the express written consent of the publisher except in the case of brief quotations embodied in critical articles and reviews.

Outskirts Press, Inc.
http://www.outskirtspress.com

ISBN: 978-1-4327-7517-9

Outskirts Press and the "OP" logo are trademarks belonging to Outskirts Press, Inc.

PRINTED IN THE UNITED STATES OF AMERICA

Acknowledgements

All the glory goes to God for His inspiration. I wish to acknowledge Steve Jaquith, former Pastor of Gospel Chapel, who allowed me to give these devotions as talks to the congregation during the Sunday morning services. My gratitude to the many mentors who by example and words showed me the way. I wish to acknowledge my beloved wife, Linda, who spent many hours editing these pages.

Table of Contents

Week 1	What is Faith?	1
Week 2	Faith and Understanding	4
Week 3	Faith Versus the Law	7
Week 4	Faith and Works	10
Week 5	Faith and Trials	13
Week 6	Faith and Courage	16
Week 7	Faith and Perseverance	19
Week 8	Faith and Suffering	22
Week 9	Faith and Overcoming Temptation	25
Week 10	Maintaining Faith	28
Week 11	Faith and Battle	32
Week 12	Faith and the Crowd	35
Week 13	Faith and Giving	38
Week 14	Faith and the Prophetic	41
Week 15	Faith and Confession	44
Week 16	Faith and Hurry	47
Week 17	Faith and Streams of Living Water	50
Week 18	Second Chance Believing	53
Week 19	Recognizing the Messiah	56
Week 20	Faith and Peace	59
Week 21	Sharing Your Faith	62
Week 22	The Goal of Our Faith	65
Week 23	Standing Firm in Your Faith	68
Week 24	Full Assurance of Faith	71
Week 25	Foundations of Faith	74
Week 26	God's Armor	77
Week 27	Faith Versus Sight	81

Week 28	Trust and Obey	84
Week 29	Seeking the Truth	87
Week 30	Jesus Came to Reveal the Father	90
Week 31	Faith and Communion	93
Week 32	Faith and Meeting Together	96
Week 33	The Kingdom Within Us	99
Week 34	Faith and Giving	102
Week 35	Waiting on God	105
Week 36	The Church	108
Week 37	God's Plan for Us	111
Week 38	True Belief	114
Week 39	Faith and Success	117
Week 40	Rest	120
Week 41	Overcoming Evil	123
Week 42	Faith Leads to the Cross	126
Week 43	Sowing Seed by Faith	129
Week 44	Faith and the Desert	132
Week 45	Following Jesus	135
Week 46	Faith and Failure	138
Week 47	Loving Our Neighbor	141
Week 48	Christians and Voting	144
Week 49	Making Your Calling Sure	147
Week 50	Fear God not Man	150
Week 51	The People God Chooses	153
Week 52	Servant or Friend	156
Week 53	Faith and Weakness	159
Week 54	Faith and Zeal	162
Week 55	Faith and Unity	165
Week 56	Faith and God's Timing	168
Week 57	Listening for God's Voice	171
Week 58	Faith and Opposition	174
Week 59	Faith and Words	177

Week 60	Faith and the Blood	180
Week 61	Faith and Your Comfort Zone	183
Week 62	Giving by Faith	186
Week 63	Multiplication	189
Week 64	Faith and Pentecost	192
Week 65	Faith and Private Thoughts	196
Week 66	Faith and Storms	199
Week 67	Faith and the Narrow Way	202
Week 68	Faith and Trouble	205
Week 69	Faith and Spiritual Intensity	208
Week 70	Faith and Doing It Over	211
Week 71	Three Conditions for Prosperity	214
Week 72	Faith and Favor	217
Week 73	Faith and Focus	220
Week 74	Faith and Deliverance	223
Week 75	Faith, Listening and Looking	226
Week 76	God's Purpose in Storms	229
Week 77	Faith and Being Sent	232
Week 78	Faith and Worship	235

Week 1

What is Faith?

For reading & meditation – Hebrews 11:1-40

"Now faith is being sure of what we hope for and certain of what we do not see." (v.1)

Living by faith is the very basis of the Christian life. The New Testament refers to many people and activities in the Old Testament where faith was exercised. We find faith mostly concealed in the Old Testament, where it is only mentioned twice. It is openly revealed in the New Testament, being mentioned over 200 times.

God says, *"the righteous will live by his faith"* (from Habakkuk 2:4; also quoted in Romans 1:17, Galatians 3:11 and Hebrews 10:38). Faith is absolutely essential. You will never make it without faith. You will neither see God nor have life. Martin Luther, the leader of the Protestant reformation, had been trying to justify himself by works and by punishing himself for his sins until he saw and believed this verse. When he received this revelation, he started a great movement of faith that is still active today.

What is faith? Hebrews 11:1 reads, *"Now faith is being sure of what we hope for and certain of what we do not see."* Faith is based on facts; it is based on truth. Here are some of the truths we need to believe by faith: God exists, and He rewards those who diligently seek Him (Hebrews 11:6); Jesus' blood shed for us on the cross cleanses us from sin (1 John 1:7); Jesus rose from the dead (1 Corinthians 15:4).

If I have faith in something that is a lie, my faith does me no good. First Corinthians 15:17 says, *"If Christ has not been raised, your faith is futile."* Although I have faith in the resurrection of Jesus, the resurrection must be true for it to have any effect.

Not every fact requires faith. In mathematics, is it faith to say that one plus one equals two? The whole of mathematics rides on that fact. The second part of the definition of faith in Hebrews is that faith is the evidence of things not seen. I can see that one plus one equals two. I can live by that. So believing in mathematics is not really faith at all.

On the other hand, I cannot prove to everyone that the blood of Jesus cleanses people from sin. Though there is evidence in people's lives, it cannot be proven. I just believe it by faith. The Bible says it; I believe it. I cannot prove it, but it is true. That is faith.

There are people who say that they will believe in God when He proves Himself to them. "Prove it first and then we will believe," they say. Even if miracles are performed, many will not believe. And even if they do believe, it may not be credited to their account with much blessing. Thomas wanted to see the nail prints of the risen Christ. Jesus showed him, but rebuked him. He said, *"Blessed are those who have not seen and yet have believed"* (John 20:29). When the rich man was in hell

WHAT IS FAITH?

asking Abraham to send him back to warn his brothers, Abraham said, *"They have Moses and the Prophets; let them listen to them. . . If they do not listen to Moses and the Prophets, they will not be convinced even if someone rises from the dead"* (see Luke 16:19-31).

For faith to be true, it must be based on facts. These facts are things that can be doubted, things that are not seen. The facts we are talking about pertain to God and what He has done for us, and how we need to respond.

Learning to live by faith is a life-long process. Each journey starts with the first step. Take a step of faith toward God, and your faith will begin to grow!

Prayer

Father, help me take a new step of faith toward You today. I pray in Jesus' name. Amen.

Week 2

Faith and Understanding

For reading & meditation – John 3: 1-21

"'How can a man be born when he is old?' Nicodemus asked. 'Surely he cannot enter a second time into his mother's womb to be born!'" (v.4)

The Christian walk is by faith. Understanding begins only when faith is exercised. Everyone has the seed of faith, but only those willing to give up their sin will ultimately allow their faith to grow.

It is possible to study the Bible and Christian religion and even teach it and become leaders, yet have no faith. This was true in Bible times and it is true today. Nicodemus, a leader of the Pharisees, came to Jesus seeking truth. Jesus said to him, *"I tell you the truth, no one can see the kingdom of God unless He is born again"* (John 3:3).

Faith comes first. Understanding follows. You could study Christianity all your life and not benefit from it. You will not even really understand it until you have faith. The kingdom

FAITH AND UNDERSTANDING

of God is entered by faith. Only those with faith in Jesus are members of it. Only those with faith in Jesus can see it and recognize it. And only those with faith in Jesus can really understand what it is all about.

Trying to understand the kingdom of God without an initial step of faith is like trying to describe calculus to someone who has not had algebra yet, or like trying to describe winter in Alaska to someone who has spent his whole life in the tropics. Although they may think they understand, they do not get it.

If you say, "Prove it to me first and then I will believe," the question is, "Will you ever believe?" It is always possible to think up an argument so you do not have to believe. Jesus said, *"If they do not listen to Moses and the Prophets, they will not be convinced even if someone rises from the dead"* (Luke 16:29). So today, though the Bible says in Psalm 19 that *"the heavens declare the glory of God; the skies proclaim the work of his hands,"* there are many who think it just happened by chance and evolved over time from simple to complex. They deny faith by making up false excuses and arguments.

Why do people not believe? Were they missing when the seed of faith was distributed? Were they ordained to be lost? I believe that God planted the seed of faith in all of us. We can all believe.

The reason they refuse to believe is because faith has demands. Habakkuk 2:4 says, *"The righteous will live by his faith."* The word "righteous" says it all. The demand is that those of faith live a righteous life. They have to stop sinning. People refuse to believe simply because they love their sin too much to stop, or they believe that their sin is too great for God to forgive, or they do not think they can stop sinning. So there is a refusal to believe, perhaps even a denial that God exists at all.

But in reality, these people do not understand the gospel.

LIVING BY FAITH

There is no sin too great for God to forgive. He even forgives over and over if we fail and come back to Him with sincere hearts of repentance. He desires from us an attitude that wants to stop sinning. He then is able to change us from within by the power of the Holy Spirit. It usually takes time, but He can and does change us. We cannot change ourselves; it does not work. These facts leave only one real excuse for nonbelievers. They love their sin too much to give it up, and faith demands that we give up our sin.

The beginning of faith can be an experiment. You decide to believe. That also involves deciding to repent of your known sins, and deciding to follow Jesus. When you do this, the door of your understanding of the gospel will just have opened. God will start to shed His light for you on the Bible as you read it. It will come alive. It will truly be like being born again.

Too many times I have met people who try to live good lives, but have no understanding of the gospel. Where is the joy, the peace, the fruit of the Spirit, or true understanding? It is absent. *"Without faith it is impossible to please God"* (Hebrews 11:6). Yet people are trying it all the time. Perhaps you are one of them. Take the step of faith. The eyes of your understanding will be opened.

Prayer

Father, help me to take steps of faith toward You so that I may understand Your gospel more perfectly. I pray in Jesus' name. Amen.

Week 3

Faith Versus the Law

For reading & meditation – Exodus 20:3-17
"you shall not..." (vs.4,7,13,14,15,16,17)

Can we be saved by keeping the law? As soon as God gave the ten commandments to Moses, the people broke them by creating a graven image (Exodus 32:8). God says that breaking the law at any one point is breaking all of it. Even when the people tried to keep the law, they could not. The apostle Paul makes it clear that although he as a Pharisee was blameless in all he did, in actuality he was not able to keep the law at all. The commandment that convicted him was the 10th: *"You shall not covet"* (Exodus 20:17). Paul realized that the law was an internal heart condition, not just an external thing. Coveting dealt with the thought life, not just external action.

Jesus took it further in the Sermon on the Mount. He called lust, an internal thing, the same as committing adultery. He called being angry with your brother, an internal thing, the same as murder, an external thing. Consequently, we may be able to fool a lot of people with our actions, when, in reality, our thoughts are sinful. Remember, God looks on the heart.

This line of reasoning caused Paul to cry out, *"What a wretched man I am! Who will rescue me from this body of death?"* (Romans 7:24). It convinced him that he was a sinner. It is enough to convince you that you are a sinner.

No one can keep the law. No one except Jesus has ever kept the law. Jesus is the only one who always obeyed with perfect heart attitude. Since we must keep the law in every part to be saved by the law, no one has ever been saved by the law. Everyone who has ever been saved, before or after Christ, was saved by faith.

If the law has never saved anyone, because they cannot keep it, why was it given? There are at least two good reasons pertinent to this discussion: 1) The law was given to show God's righteous standard; 2) The law was given to convict us that we could not keep God's righteous standard and we needed help.

More than 400 years prior to the law being given, *"Abraham believed God and God credited it to him as righteousness"* (Romans 4:3). Before the law was given, salvation was by faith. After the law was given and before Christ's atoning sacrifice, salvation was also by faith. Hebrews eleven, the faith chapter, speaks of the heroes of faith who lived after the law but before Christ. And, of course, since Christ, all are saved only by faith in Him. The only logical conclusion we can draw from this is that Christ's blood is able to save mankind from the beginning of time to its end. From Adam to the end of the age, it is only by faith in Christ that anyone is saved. Now some may not understand what God's provision is, having never heard, or having lived before it happened, but they still need to believe that God has made a way, has made a provision that will separate us from our sin and free us to enter His presence forever.

FAITH VERSUS THE LAW

What is the importance of the law with respect to faith? Jesus kept the law. That made His blood acceptable to atone or pay for our sins. We trust Jesus, identifying with Him in his death, by faith. Then when God the Father looks at us, He sees Jesus. By faith, we are perfect in Jesus, always keeping the law. Although we do not see that completely worked out here on earth, He is changing us. One day we will be totally perfected in body and soul as well as spirit, when we step into His presence forever.

No self-effort will get you anywhere with God. You cannot keep the law. Any pummeling of the body by yourself has no effect on changing your inner sinful nature. It is only by faith that we can receive forgiveness of sins and be granted repentance. God is the one who changes us on the inside. When we are changed, we will find that the law is written on our hearts. We keep it automatically without trying. That is what happens to those who are walking in the Spirit.

You must believe that *"God ... exists and that He rewards those who earnestly seek Him"* (Hebrews 11:6). Diligently seek Him. Regularly pray. Regularly read the Bible. Regularly have fellowship with other believers. Regularly reflect on your inner life and repent. Then just live your life, and watch it grow in Him.

Prayer

Father, thank You that You took care of all my sins on the cross. Help me to allow You to change me from within. I pray in Jesus' name. Amen.

Week 4

Faith and Works

For reading & meditation – James 2:14-26

"As the body without the spirit is dead, so faith without deeds is dead." (v.26)

Works cannot save you; only faith in Jesus can. If you have faith, you will prove it by your works. Faith demands action. Those with faith do the acts of faith, because they believe in and love God. Consequently, faith and works always show up together. Your faith is proved by what you do.

Only faith makes us righteous. We cannot please God without faith. Our deeds do not make us righteous. In James 2, we see those deeds cropping up again. They need to be put in the right perspective. Faith always results in deeds. We act because we have faith. We prove we have faith by our actions.

Giving is a prime example. If we gave a tithe to get God to think well of us, that would be the wrong attitude. We would be trying to justify ourselves by a work. It would result in condemnation. If, on the other hand, we believe that God cares

FAITH AND WORKS

for His children, and we believe that God will never leave us or forsake us and that He promises to take care of our needs, then giving a tithe or more is an easy, joyous thing to do. We can give because we believe God will meet our need. In fact, our giving proves our faith when done in this manner.

Faith demands action. We believe God cares for us. Therefore, we can stop being as self-centered and start looking to the needs of others. Matthew 6:33 says, *"But seek first his kingdom and his righteousness, and all these things will be given to you as well."* The phrase, *"all these things"* refers to the necessities of life. If we believe and do nothing, does God have to act to honor our faith? He says to "seek" His kingdom and His righteousness. If we believe, we need to obey. It is a principle. Faith principles are all action principles. You prove your faith by implementing them. In doing so, you are showing trust in God.

If you had no faith, it would not make sense to do what faith demands. The world says to love self first, promote self first; if you don't, who will? Faith, on the other hand, says to love your neighbor as yourself, to give honor where honor is due. Do this because you believe that God will take care of you, even if you have to sacrifice for someone else. So faith proves itself in action.

In Rahab's story, James says she was saved by what she did. Hebrews 11:31 says she was saved by faith. James 2 uses Abraham's story to show that he was saved by what he did. In Romans 4, Paul uses Abraham's story to show that he was justified by faith. Who is right? They both are! It is faith resulting in action that saves. How does one know he has faith if it is not acted on?

If you believe the gospel, then the action that faith demands is that you show it to the world by being baptized. Faith

LIVING BY FAITH

demands that you repent of your sins, that you covenant in your heart to stop sinning. Faith demands that you look for ways to love others. Faith demands that you take the risk of standing up for what is right. There are lots of demands of faith. They all take action. They all involve risk. But you do them because you have faith. It is faith that gives you the courage to do what you could not do without it.

We obey because we can trust God. We serve Him because we love Him, and not because we want to appease Him. So, yes, there are works, but they are done as a result of faith.

Prayer

Father, I want my faith to result in action. Help that to come about in my life. In Jesus' name I pray. Amen.

Week 5

Faith and Trials

For reading & meditation – James 1:2-18

"Consider it pure joy, my brothers, whenever you face trials of many kinds, because you know that the testing of your faith develops perseverance. Perseverance must finish its work so that you may be mature and complete, not lacking anything." (vs.2-4)

Trials always have a purpose. The attitude with which you go through them makes all the difference. James says, *"Consider it pure joy"* when you are faced with a trial. Is he asking the impossible? This is not usually the way we face our trials. We tend to do so with fear and trepidation. Or, in the midst of them, we try to get out of them any way we can. You can have joy and many other emotions all at the same time because, after all, it is a trial.

Many years ago when I was lying paralyzed on a hospital bed in Manila, God filled me with joy and peace like I had never had before. My circumstances did not look very good. My dad, who was suffering with Alzheimer's disease 9000 miles away, was so confused by the news, he thought I had died. My trial was not just my trial, but a trial for my family and all those who depended on me. I was visited by many, and received many cards and encouragements. Others went through this with varying emotions. My wife, bless her heart, drove an hour and a half each way through incredible traffic every day to come see me during the two weeks I was there. She never complained. Some who visited me were almost in mourning, thinking that I would soon pass on. It was a wonderful, horrible trial.

When you have a trial, you can choose how you will respond. God says to respond with joy. Here is why. God has a plan for all Christians on earth. That plan is to conform them to the image of Christ (Romans 8:29). He is going to mold your character into that of Christ. You cannot take your body with you when you die, but you will take your character, so that is what God wants to change into His image. When your character is conformed to His image, you will be much more effective in His service.

The primary instrument God uses to change your character is trials. He puts you in all the situations of life. He knows about them all in advance. They will either make you bitter, or they will make you better. It all depends on how you go through them. Is your attitude one of faith, believing that God is on the throne of your life? Is it one of believing that He only wants good things for you? Is it one of believing that good will come out of every trial? Is it one of believing that character development into the image of Christ is the most important thing that can happen to you? If it is, than you can thank God for your trials. You can praise Him for them. You can be ecstatic with joy in the midst of them, because you are being conformed to His image.

FAITH AND TRIALS

It is only in the fire that gold is purified. Someone asked a silver smith when he knew it was time to remove the silver from the fire. His answer was, "When I can see my face in it." In the same way, God will keep allowing us to go through trials until we are done, until He can see His image in us.

The whole of scripture documents trials of many great men and women of faith. These were written as encouragement to us. Not all of them passed all their tests, and we will not pass all of ours either. But God never gives up on us. We have been predestined to be conformed to His image. He is going to complete the refining process for each one of us.

So, when trials overwhelm you, when nothing seems to be going your way, rejoice in Jesus. Move, rest, and act in His peace and joy. It is an exercise of your faith to do this. But the results will be well worth it. God is working on us for our good through our trials.

PRAYER

Thank You, Father, for my many trials. Help me to rejoice in my next one, knowing that You are refining me. I pray in Jesus' name. Amen.

Week 6

Faith and Courage

For reading & meditation – 1 Samuel 17:1-51

"Let no one lose heart on account of this Philistine; your servant will go and fight him." (v.32)

Courage is defined in the dictionary as the quality of mind which meets opposition or danger with calmness, firmness, and intrepidity; the quality of being fearless; or bravery. In other words, in order to show courage, there must be some danger or opposition. There must be risk. You may be putting your life or your reputation on the line.

Some people put their lives on the line foolishly. That is not courage. There must be something of great value that gives you a reason for courage. What is worth dying for? Is faith or freedom or truth worth dying for? Is it worth living for? Would you deliberately put yourself in that place of risk if you were called upon to do it?

The Bible is full of stories of people who exhibited great courage. Some were spared, but some gave their lives. Daniel knew of the king's decree that anyone who prayed to any God except the king for the next thirty days would be thrown into the lions' den. He exhibited courage in completely ignoring this decree and praying as he always had: three times per day. God spared him. David risked everything in facing Goliath. It was his faith that led him to do it. He looked to God, not at the enemy. This explains some of his great successes later on. Before each battle, he had the habit of inquiring of the Lord. The Lord would speak some instructions into his heart, and he would obey them. Consequently, whether with few or with many, he was always victorious. The apostles, when released from prison, were told not to preach in Jesus' name. Peter and John replied, *"Judge for yourselves whether it is right in God's sight to obey you rather than God. For we cannot help speaking about what we have seen and heard"* (Acts 4:19-20). As a result of their continued speaking, the apostle James was martyred. Peter was arrested and scheduled for execution when he was miraculously released from prison.

Without courage resulting from faith, the gospel would never have spread as it did. Without courage, Christianity as we know it would never have succeeded. With the power of the Holy Spirit living in you, and faith in the living God, you, too, can take courage and advance the gospel, even amidst opposition.

In the world today, the places where the gospel is having the most effect is where the opposition is the strongest. In 1949 all the western missionaries were driven out of China by the communists. At the time, there were perhaps a total of 80,000 Christians in the country. Many of those Christians were somewhat nominal, and depended on the faith of the missionaries rather than their own faith. When the missionaries left, many thought that the church in China was doomed. Thirty years later, at the end of the cultural revolution, when China started opening to foreigners again, there was a shock waiting. The church, amid much opposition, had grown from a few thousand to almost as many millions. What happened? During opposition, the true believers took courage and risked everything to stay Christian and to spread the good news of Christ. Many were martyred, but many more believed. The same thing is happening today in various parts of the world, such as North Korea.

In the USA, I think the greatest opposition is from apathy. Many people just do not think faith is important, because life is easy. Consequently, we do not see very much courage. If we do not stand up boldly against this apathetic darkness, our ease of life will be eroded. Then, the church will be forced to become strong.

You have the Holy Spirit. You have faith. Exercise it courageously in every situation in your life now. Live righteously and openly before all men now, with no compromise. It will make a huge difference. Many characters in the Bible exhibited courage in standing up for their faith regardless of consequences and dangers. Some were spared and some not, but all were overcomers. Be an overcomer!

Prayer

Father, help me be courageous enough to stand for righteousness in every situation in my life. I pray this in Jesus' name. Amen.

Week 7

Faith and Perseverance

For reading & meditation – Psalm 91

"For he will command his angels concerning you to guard you in all your ways." (v.11)

Psalm 57 expresses David's thoughts as he was running from Saul, who was trying to catch and kill him: *"Have mercy on me, O God, have mercy on me, for in you my soul takes refuge… I cry out to God Most High, to God, who fulfills his purpose for me. He sends from heaven and saves me, rebuking those who hotly pursue me… Be exalted, O God, above the heavens; let your glory be over all the earth."*

David's situation did not look good. From a worldly point of view, it looked like his career was over before it started. But David had a different point of view. He knew that God had put a call on his life. He knew that God had work He wanted him to do. Not only did he know it, he proclaimed it in the midst of his waiting. When things were at the lowest, he said, *"I cry out to God…who fulfills his purpose for me."* Then he began to praise God.

When God allows us to enter a time of testing, we usually are not told how long the test will last or how painful it will be. We only know for sure that it will be long enough and hard enough to test us. God never allows us to go through a trial that would, with His help, be too hard for us to take. *"God is faithful; he will not let you be tempted beyond what you can bear. But when you are tempted, he will also provide a way out so that you can stand up under it"* (1 Corinthians 10:13). He will give us enough grace for each trial.

We can learn from David how to persevere successfully in our trials. **First**, he acknowledged that he was in a trial. It is important to admit your problems to God. Notice, however, that this acknowledgement was not a complaint.

Second, David cried out to God for mercy. He reminded God of His promises. He took refuge in God. Let us follow his example. Psalm 91 offers promises of rescue, of freedom from fear, and of escape from the punishment of the wicked.

Third, he believed God for the fulfillment of the purpose that God had given him. God had promised him the kingdom. God has also given you purpose. He has works prepared for you to do for Him. In the midst of trial, you can start thanking Him that He fully intends to accomplish through you all that He has purposed for you. In the midst of trial, we need to focus on what God has said, and believe Him for fulfillment.

Fourth, David began to praise God in the midst of his situation. Beginning early in the morning, he remained steadfast in praising God for what God was doing and would do in the future.

If we stand strong in faith in the midst of trials, like David did, we will persevere until the trial is over and our situation changes. Then we will be able to look back and thank God

FAITH AND PERSEVERENCE

for taking us through the difficult time. So acknowledge the trial. Cry out for mercy. Believe God for the fulfillment of your calling. And, finally, begin to praise God in the midst of the situation. When you do these things, as did David, you will eventually experience success in fulfilling your calling.

Prayer

Father, make me strong in the midst of trials. Help me to stand on the promises in the Bible. I pray in Jesus' name. Amen.

Week 8

Faith and Suffering

For reading & meditation – Ephesians 6:11-18

"...take up the shield of faith, with which you can extinguish all the flaming arrows of the evil one." (v.16)

Jesus was made perfect in suffering. *"Although he was a son, he learned obedience from what he suffered"* (Hebrews 5:8). He endured suffering all the way through His ministry from being rejected at Nazareth to the death on the cross. Jesus said, *"If they persecuted me, they will persecute you also"* (John 15:20). Scripture says: *"In fact, everyone who wants to live a godly life in Christ Jesus will be persecuted"* (2 Timothy 3:12).

Jesus was persecuted. You will be persecuted if you choose to follow Him. Jesus suffered. You will suffer if you choose to follow Him. He said in Luke 21:17, *"All men will hate you because of me."*

We are not talking about illnesses and accidents here. They will also come because we live in a fallen world. What we are talking about is suffering because we stand against the worldly

FAITH AND SUFFERING

system in our culture all around us, because we stand up and stand out for Jesus. Jesus said it would come. Expect it.

There really is no choice. If you want to live your life to avoid persecution and suffering, I have bad news for you. If you do not suffer now, it will be a lot worse later. There will come a time when you wished you had taken a stand for Jesus. So stand firm in your faith all the way to the end. In fact, the verse quoted from Luke 21 above is expanded in Matthew 10:22 to say, *"All men will hate you because of me, but he who stands firm to the end will be saved."*

So the question arises: Since we can expect to be persecuted for our faith, what should we do to prepare for this coming persecution? I have several suggestions. **First:** find out about those around the world who are already suffering greatly for their faith. Our brothers and sisters in communist countries, Muslim areas, and Hindu areas are the primary ones that come to mind. Our fellow Christians are having their earthly goods unjustly taken, being put in prison without cause, and being martyred daily for their faith. Find out about them. Pray for them. As opportunity arises, help them in other ways.

Second: Deepen your faith. Take responsibility not only to learn all you can about God and His ways, but also to seek Him diligently, to know Him and follow Him with your whole heart. Arm yourself with the full armor of God found in Ephesians 6. Become a wholehearted disciple.

Third: Welcome opposition. In the book of Acts, the apostles rejoiced that they were counted worthy to suffer for Jesus. People opposed Jesus. If you are becoming like Him, they will oppose you, too. Just make sure it is because you are living a godly life in Jesus that you are suffering, and not because of your own sin.

Fourth: Realize that it is where people suffer for Jesus that the greatest gains are being made in this world for the kingdom of God. If you are not a threat to the enemy, he will leave you alone. It is only if you are pushing back his kingdom of darkness that he is going to fight back. Trouble may mean that you are doing something right.

Pray for the persecuted church. Become a better disciple of Christ than you are now. Welcome suffering for Christ when it comes. Realize that you would not be undergoing opposition if you were not pushing back the darkness. Rejoice, for the greatest gains for the kingdom come where there is persecution.

Prayer

Father, help me stand against evil regardless of the cost. Help me to love everyone. I pray in Jesus' name. Amen.

Week 9
Faith and Overcoming Temptation

For reading and meditation – Hebrews 3:7-19

"But encourage one another daily, as long as it is called Today, so that none of you may be hardened by sin's deceitfulness" (v.13)

Jesus had victory over every temptation and sin while He was on earth. *"For we do not have a high priest who is unable to sympathize with our weaknesses, but we have one who has been tempted in every way, just as we are -- yet was without sin"* (Hebrews 4:15). To me this verse is amazing. How could anyone resist every temptation? I find that sometimes I resist hard temptations and win; but sometimes I hardly even resist lesser temptations and lose. I was born with a sin nature, and it is still possible for me to choose it over the new nature. Jesus was able to resist every temptation perfectly for his entire lifetime on earth. Wow!

If Jesus perfectly resisted, then He is our pattern. First John 1:6-9 shows us how. It reads, *"If we claim to have fellowship with him yet walk in the darkness, we lie and do not live by the truth. But if we walk in the light, as he is in the light, we have fellowship with one another, and the blood of Jesus, his Son, purifies us from* all sin. *If we claim to be without sin, we deceive ourselves and the truth is not in us. If we confess our sins, he is faithful and just and will forgive us our sins and purify us from all unrighteousness.*"

The **first** step in overcoming temptation is to walk in the light rather than in darkness. When the Holy Spirit lives within us and we maintain communication and fellowship with Him in our hearts, and walk in His peace, we are walking in the light. When we listen to the urgings of the Holy Spirit to act or to cease from acting and we obey, then we are walking in the light. When we deliberately do something we think is wrong or we are convicted is wrong, or we know is contrary to scripture, we sin. When we continue to knowingly walk in that sin without repentance, we are walking in darkness.

For sin to be forgiven we must bring it into the light rather than hide it in our hearts. We must agree that it is sin. We must decide to stop doing it, and go God's way instead. What a great thing: God through Jesus forgives us!

By faith we believe that it is important to live righteously. God is perfecting us. He is changing us, but it is a slow process with many tests and trials, with many failings. How do we keep from stumbling so much?

Our faith keeps us from falling. We walk in the light by faith. Walking in the light is a continual process. Maintain the presence of God in your life continually. Tune your heart to Him in the morning when you arise and maintain His presence throughout the day. Even when you are doing other things, you can practice being aware of God's presence.

God never tempts anyone. If we are focusing on Him, it will be harder for a temptation to make its way to our conscious minds. But when it does, we can bring it immediately to the light with a prayer for strengthening. Then God will help us overcome it. *"God is faithful; he will not let you be tempted*

FAITH AND OVERCOMING TEMPTATION

beyond what you can bear. But when you are tempted, he will also provide a way out so that you can stand up under it" (I Corinthians 10:13). Jesus met temptation with scripture quickened by the Spirit. He can do the same for you, by bringing to you the scripture you need in order to overcome.

Even though we purpose to continuously walk in the light, we will sometimes fall into temptation. That is when we need the **second** step, confession. When we confess, we are saying we do not want this sin to have a part of our heart. We put it out and turn it over to Jesus, and He forgives it. Then we are back to walking in the light. We need to do this by faith, and quickly, when we fall. A war has many battles. Some are won and some are lost, but we are always given another chance when we confess from the heart, regardless of the grievousness of the sin. The important thing about confession is that it needs to be sincerely from the heart. God is looking at your heart.

As you continue walking in the light and growing in faith, you will find that you are becoming stronger in that area that used to be so bothersome. You will be an overcomer. Sometimes it is just a matter of deciding who you really want to serve: Jesus and your new nature, or the devil and your old nature. Faith will always point you to serving Jesus.

Walk in the light. Practice the presence of God every day. When temptation comes, run to Jesus for help. But if you do fall into temptation, quickly confess and renounce your sin from the heart. Jesus will forgive and reinstate you. Through this process, you will become strong in Him.

Prayer

Father, help me stay close enough to Jesus so that I am not easily tempted. When I give in to temptation, help me to quickly repent and step back into the light. I pray in Jesus' name. Amen.

Week 10

Maintaining Faith

For reading & meditation – Psalm 8
"When I consider your heavens, the work of your fingers, the moon and the stars, which you have set in place..." (v.3)

There are primarily two things that cause young people to lose their faith. I heard an astounding statistic: fifty percent of U.S. students who have faith upon entering college lose it by graduation. This is not the historical trend in America, and it must be stopped.

The main cause for this loss of faith is sexual immorality. The Bible takes a strong stance against this: *"Flee from sexual immorality. All other sins a man commits are outside his body, but he who sins sexually sins against his own body"* (1 Corinthians 6:18). Jesus said in the sermon on the mount, *"But I tell you that anyone who looks at a woman lustfully has already committed adultery with her in his heart"* (Matthew 5:28).

Students are vulnerable, away from home and parents for the first time, and it is easy for them to get caught in the trap of lust and pornography. If this deadly addiction is allowed to have its way, it will destroy faith. If you are caught in this trap, run, do not walk, to get help! It is nearly impossible to overcome by yourself.

Take steps to avoid falling into sexual immorality. Eliminate from your life all the media and anything you own that tempts you sexually. This may seem harsh, but we are talking about your eternal soul. Make a vow of faithfulness to your life partner, whether or not you presently have one.

As Christians we are called to stand in contrast to the world, living a pure and clean life before all. This stand will bring you persecution, when you refuse to go to that movie or watch that show or participate in other sexually tempting behaviors. But to follow Christ, you must take this stand. It will cause you to be called names, but it will glorify God and bring you a reward. For you who are still young, the battle will only increase when you get away from home. Prepare now!

The other thing that causes young people to lose their faith is naturalistic thinking. Naturalistic reasoning, which permeates most universities today, eliminates all supernatural explanations. John 1:3 says, *"Through him all things were made; without him nothing was made that has been made."* Colossians 1:17 says, *"He is before all things, and in him all things hold together."*

The Bible makes it clear that all explanations must include a supernatural element. He holds everything together. If we try to explain anything without God, we will always fall short. He must be included in every explanation. This makes it tough in schools where God is ignored.

If you bring God into your explanations, you will be discriminated against. Your grade may be lowered. You might fail the course. When I was in college in 1968, I had just been baptized in the Holy Spirit and had just read the book, "They Speak with Other Tongues" by John Sherrill. I met another student walking across the college campus with the same book in his hand. I started a conversation with him. He said that they used that book in his sociology course as an example of aberrant behavior, explaining it psychologically.

To succeed at a secular university, you must be prepared to do battle against naturalistic explanations in many of your courses. It will be hard, and you must prepare yourself prior to going. Get into the Bible and get the Bible into you. Develop discernment so you can tell when the explanations are contrary to the truth. Even at many Christian universities, secular naturalistic philosophies have been allowed to permeate many courses. These must be detected and opposed.

Any explanation that omits God is incomplete. Incomplete explanations are okay, as long as they are recognized as only partial. The trouble comes when the explanation clearly opposes the truth, denying God as an option.

The danger of naturalistic philosophy is that it is expounded everywhere. In some fields, it is the only acceptable professional philosophy. For certain directions in life, you will either have to do battle to continue (and we need some champions to do that) or you will give in to the philosophy and lose your faith. College is an intellectual environment. If only naturalistic philosophy is given out from this environment, then many will be persuaded that it must be right.

Remember that Jesus Christ holds everything together. He is Lord of the universe. Nothing happens without His consent. He is involved in everything. There are no totally naturalistic explanations. Prepare to do battle in this area and deal with the opposition that comes.

In summary, to survive college with your faith intact, be

prepared to do battle against sexual immorality and against naturalistic philosophy. Commit yourselves to purity. Learn and believe the scriptures. Keep your faith strong by committing yourself to practice it openly and regularly wherever God leads you. We need to arm ourselves in these areas because the battle will be difficult. But with faithfulness and perseverance we can succeed.

Prayer

Father, help me to adequately prepare for the task ahead in the battles for morality and truth. I pray in Jesus' name. Amen.

Week 11

Faith and Battle

For Reading & Meditation – Ephesians 6:10-20

"Put on the full armor of God so that you can take your stand against the devil's schemes." (v.11)

We battle against unseen spiritual forces in this dark world. We battle for people. These are the two parts to the battle. The enemy forces hold people in darkness. They blind their eyes. They keep them from believing the gospel. So we must defeat them with our testimony, with the word, with prayer, with the blood of Jesus and with our willingness to lay down our lives for the cause. When the enemy is defeated, the gospel will more readily penetrate the hearts of people and be believed. We must also intercede for people.

We need to realize that we are currently in the midst of the battle. All Christians are already enlisted. The results of this battle are the eternal destinies of people. The eternal destiny of someone depends on you.

We must battle against the enemy. Ephesians 6:12 says,

FAITH AND BATTLE

"For our struggle is not against flesh and blood, but against the rulers, against the authorities, against the powers of this dark world and against the spiritual forces of evil in the heavenly realms." Although Satan was defeated at the cross, he still has influence in this world. Revelation 12:11 says, *"They overcame him by the blood of the Lamb and by the word of their testimony; they did not love their lives so much as to shrink from death."*

This verse from Revelation gives us three ways to defeat Satan. First, we need to be really solid in our **position** in Christ. Jesus took all our sin and, regardless of the temptations we face, we should maintain His covering, staying in Him and resistant to temptation.

Secondly, we should maintain words that are a **testimony**. Jesus wants to change us into His likeness. The closer to Him we come, the more like Him we will be. Our words in the world, not just in the church, need to be a constant testimony of who we are in Christ and what He has done for us.

Thirdly, our faith needs to be strong enough so that we **do not shrink** from death and loss of other kinds. There has been too much compromise in our society, in our lives. We have refused to stand up for our morals in the face of loss and danger. The great heroes of the Bible stood up in the face of danger. Joseph would not compromise with Potipher's wife, and suffered years of prison time. Daniel refused to stop praying publicly, and they tried to execute him for it. Let us also stand up in the face of danger.

We need to reckon ourselves dead to the world in Christ. We died when He died. Our home is in heaven. What we do now on earth is more like moving our game piece around the board. Our real life is in heaven, not here. Do not compromise eternal life for an earthly reward. It is not worth it.

We need to do battle for all people, saved and lost. No one

is now beyond God's reach. Jesus loves everyone. Jesus died for everyone. People who do not yet know Jesus have a veil over their eyes. They are blinded to the truth. The enemy is the one who does this blinding. Our prayers against the enemy are like artillery, softening up the ground so people will believe when they hear the gospel.

We battle for people in at least three ways. We battle for people with our **prayers**. God hears and answers our prayers. We must believe this. Sharpen up your prayer life. If you do not pray for your loved ones and neighbors, who will? We battle for people with our **actions**. We need to live clean, pure lives before the world. This can only be done if we truly are clean on the inside. When we are clean on the inside, our deeds of charity will have a multiplied effect. Finally, we do battle for people with our **words**. Words are last for a reason. When I was younger, we called it witnessing when we used our words. If we pray, getting closer to Jesus, our words will have a much more potent effect.

There are many people who have heard the gospel, but it has not had its needed impact on them yet. They are waiting to see someone who is living it. Will you be that someone?

By faith we need to do battle in this world to bring about the kingdom. Let us do battle against the enemy and let us do battle for people. The battle is here. Will you be a good soldier?

Prayer

Father, help me to fight against the devil and for people in ways that will increase your kingdom. I pray in Jesus' name. Amen.

Week 12

Faith and the Crowd

For reading and meditation – Ezekiel 9:1-11

"Go throughout the city of Jerusalem and put a mark on the foreheads of those who grieve and lament over all the detestable things that are done in it." (v.4)

How much does the crowd influence you? Jesus said, *"Enter through the narrow gate. For wide is the gate and broad is the road that leads to destruction, and many enter through it. But small is the gate and narrow the road that leads to life, and only a few find it"* (Matthew 7:13-14). This scripture startled me when I was a teenager. In my hometown, everyone seemed to be religious. Everyone I knew went to church somewhere. I said to myself, "If all these people think they are on the road to life, and I think I am on the road to life, something must be amiss. Most people, according to this passage, are not on the road to life. I am not even sure I am on it." After that thought, I made a decision: I would seek the road to life until I found it for sure. During that time of seeking, I would keep my mouth shut.

Once I found the road that leads to life, I would tell people about it.

It was several years before I knew I was on the road to life. Romans 8:16 says, *"The Spirit himself testifies with our spirit that we are God's children."* We know we are on the road to life when the Holy Spirit bears witness of it to us. I cannot tell you exactly when I was saved, but I can tell you when I first knew it for sure in my heart. It took several more years before I really started telling people about it. God had to change me before He could use me to affect others.

The crowd will always take the easiest way. Those people who follow the crowd will say, "I am not so bad; everyone does it," when trying to justify a questionable lifestyle choice. They will order their life by popular culture rather than by God's standards. The crowd says, "There are many roads to God; you just need to be sincere." The crowd is on its way to hell!

To make it to heaven, to enter the kingdom, to become a Christian, you must separate yourself from the crowd. You must not evaluate yourself by the crowd, but by the Bible. You must not do things just because they are acceptable in society. Kingdom people cannot run with the world's crowd. In the kingdom, the standards do not change. Divorce and adultery are still sins in the kingdom. Selfishness is still a sin in the kingdom. You must get out of the crowd.

There is another crowd to avoid. If you want to become all God wants you to become, you need to get out of the crowd of Christians who think they have already arrived. You need to get out of the crowd of Christians who are compromising their values. You need to get out of the crowd of Christians who are following the world. To move on with Christ, stop getting your advice from ungodly people. Start doing things that ungodly people would never advise. Meditate on scripture. Pray. Listen

FAITH AND THE CROWD

to and obey the leadings of the Holy Spirit.

Spend your spare time with God, building your relationship. Then, when your fellowship is sweet, listen, and do what He tells you. Make the rest of your life a ministry, too: your work, your family time, your transportation time, your shopping time. Believe that God put you on earth with a purpose for the kingdom, and not for your own pleasure. *"Seek first His kingdom and His righteousness"* (Matthew 6:33). The crowd will never do that!

Individually, you stand or fall before the judgment seat of Christ. Only by removing yourself from the crowd and its standards will you be successful. We need to judge ourselves only by scripture, and not by the norms of our wider culture. We need to set the standard for others to follow, not be swayed by the crowd.

There are many others on the road to life. You will find them everywhere. When you are putting Jesus first, others on the same road will become obvious to you. They are not walking the broad path with the crowd. They have come out of the crowd, like you have, and brought others with them into true life.

Prayer

Father, I have followed the crowd too much. I repent. Help me to follow you wholeheartedly. In Jesus' name I pray. Amen

------ Week 13 ------

Faith and Giving

For reading and meditation – 2 Corinthians 9:6-15

"Remember this: Whoever sows sparingly will also reap sparingly, and whoever sows generously will also reap generously. Each man should give what he has decided in his heart to give, not reluctantly or under compulsion, for God loves a cheerful giver. And God is able to make all grace abound to you, so that in all things at all times, having all that you need, you will abound in every good work." (vs.6-8)

When you give, you will be a reaper of what you sow. You will reap more than you sow. You will reap later than you sow. You will reap in proportion to what you sow. If you tithe, God promises to meet your needs. Give, and it will be given to you in abundance.

There are two spiritual principles at work in giving. Since they are spiritual principles, it takes faith to believe them. People do not give the way they should because they lack faith in God's spiritual principles. If we have faith in what is written in the Bible, we will show it by our actions in giving.

The first principle of giving is the principle of sowing and reaping. When we sow for the kingdom of God, we also become reapers of what we sow. When we sow financially, we reap in accordance with how we sow. If we sow sparingly, we reap sparingly. If we sow abundantly, we reap abundantly.

The principle of sowing and reaping has several aspects. There is a time for sowing. Now is the time to sow into the kingdom. If we believe the above verse, we should sow as abundantly as we can, cheerfully and not under compulsion.

The second part of the sowing and reaping cycle is the time in between the sowing and reaping. It is a time that demands patience. After sowing, the farmer continues to water and weed. The sun and warmth need to be allowed to do their work as the sown seed grows. For many of us, a lot of what has been sown in the past is now in this stage. We do not see a whole lot of fruit yet, but we are trusting God for the harvest yet to come.

Finally, there is a reaping. You always reap more than you sow. Reaping may not even come in this lifetime, but be assured it will come. There will be a reaping for everything that you ever sowed for the gospel. We need to be patient with prayerful diligence and not lose heart. Then we will persevere to the time of harvest.

The second principle of giving is the principle of tithing. Malachi 3:10 says, *"'Bring the whole tithe into the storehouse, that there may be food in my house. Test me in this,' says the* Lord *Almighty, 'and see if I will not throw open the floodgates of heaven and pour out so much blessing that you will not have room enough for it.'"* When we tithe, God promises to take care of our financial needs here and now, not just adequately, but abundantly! The abundance will be so great that there will not even be room for it.

We have two things to believe when we give. **First**, we need to believe that what we give to God will really advance the kingdom of God. What we sow in giving is temporal and earthly. What we reap is eternal and heavenly. What we do here on earth will make a difference for eternity. We need to believe that. **Second**, we need to believe that God will take care of our needs if we give to Him first. He promises that He will. If we overcome our fears and believe, we will make tithing the beginning place of our giving. As God proves Himself by supplying our needs when we tithe, we will begin to give more than a tithe.

What you give is a matter of trust. Do you believe what it says about giving in the Bible? You prove your belief by acting on it. If you do not act, you will never even test God to allow Him to prove that He fulfills His promises. Give as much as you can give cheerfully to the works of God. I guarantee that you will be glad you did. I have never regretted giving. Neither will you.

Prayer

Father, help me to become an abundant giver. Show me where to give and help me to give cheerfully. I pray in Jesus' name.
Amen.

Week 14

Faith and the Prophetic

For reading and meditation – Mark 4:35-41
"Even the wind and the waves obey him!" (v.41)

One night I heard the Lord speak my name. It is strange that His voice sounded a lot like my pastor's son. Anyway, the Lord got my attention. I was seeing the ocean surface from high above it. There were some large waves heading out. That was all, but it got me thinking about waves.

As a science teacher, I know that regular ocean waves have three factors that influence their formation: the speed of the wind, the duration of the wind, and the size of the ocean. The harder the wind blows, the bigger the waves will be. The longer the wind blows over the water, the more intense the waves will be. The bigger the ocean, the more regular the waves will be.

Wind is a type of the Holy Spirit. Our lives are like waves of the sea. As the wind of the Holy Spirit blows intensely on our lives for long periods of time, our lives start to line up in conformity with Christ. The more intensely He blows on us, the bigger will be our effect on our world.

There is another way that waves are formed. This second method is, I believe, the kind of wave that I saw in the vision. When there is a shifting of the earth under the sea (an earthquake), a giant wave called a *tsunami* is formed. When a tsunami is coming, you do not go down to the beach to watch like you would for a wave caused by the wind. You hasten to higher ground, as the wave may be up to 200 feet from trough to crest. Tsunamis are rare, but deadly. They are caused by a shifting of the earth, not merely by the wind.

The tsunami I saw was still out at sea with no land in sight. But it is coming, and we need to prepare. We can no longer be spectators to the waves on the beach, as we could with wind-driven waves. For the spectators and sunbathers, those who are comfortable in their pews, there will be devastation. The world will only see devastation. It will look like the church is coming apart. But in actuality, just the opposite will be happening to the true church of Jesus Christ.

The Spirit of God is moving over the earth, and has been for a long time. The intensity of the wind is increasing. God is preparing the ground for the harvest. We are those who are called to catch this harvest. Now is the time for us to prepare. When the harvest comes, following the tsunami, it will be time to gather, not time to prepare. We can expect an awesome harvest.

After Jesus had spoken from Simon's boat, He said to him, *"'Put out into deep water, and let down the nets for a catch'… When they had done so, they caught such a large number of fish that their nets began to break… For he and all his companions were astonished at the catch of fish they had taken"* (see Luke 5:1-11). Simon had no catch all night, and then, all of a sudden, there was a huge, astonishing catch. It seems that we have also fished all night with little result. That is about to change. There is an awesome and astonishing harvest being prepared that will be brought in when the tsunami of the Spirit hits.

The harvest demands that there be harvesters. Every available person needs to make him or herself ready to be used when the time is ripe. Be ready in season and out of season, for we will not have much warning when the actual time comes. The harvest will be very large, but, as in all harvests, the time of harvest will also be short. The day of opportunity will arrive but it will not last forever. The window will open and we need to be ready to act immediately to catch the harvest, because the time will come when the window of opportunity will again close.

The shift in the earth has already taken place. The tsunami has already been loosed, but is out at sea. It is coming. Get ready! It is by faith that we believe that we live in the most awesome of times. The appearance of the tsunami will not be in the form that we expect. Jesus never seems to come that way. So let the wind of the Spirit blow over you. Align your life with His. Find the ministry that He has for you. Tune your ear to hear His voice. Get ready to catch the harvest. Believe it is coming. Prove that you believe the harvest is coming by preparing now.

Prayer

Father, I want to be ready to help catch the harvest when it comes. Help me to prepare now. I pray in Jesus' name. Amen.

Week 15

Faith and Confession

For reading and meditation - Romans 10:5-13

"That if you confess with your mouth, 'Jesus is LORD,' and believe in your heart that God raised him from the dead, you will be saved." (v.9)

What is in your heart will come out of your mouth. Do you listen to yourself? What you really believe about anything and everything will make its way out your mouth. Jesus said in Matthew 12:34-37, *"out of the overflow of the heart the mouth speaks. The good man brings good things out of the good stored up in him, and the evil man brings evil things out of the evil stored up in him. But I tell you that men will have to give an account on the day of judgment for every careless word they have spoken. For by your words you will be acquitted, and by your words you will be condemned."*

It is good to listen to our own talk, not the polished talk we do when we want to look good, but how we talk when we are in an informal setting and can say anything. Jesus called it "every careless word." We all have careless words. What is your confession when your guard is down? Do you listen?

Sometimes an unexpected difficulty arises and we are tempted to release words that are not of faith. We need to remember that we have faith, and release words accordingly. The bigger the problem, the bigger the faith we need. We have faith. We have confessed that Jesus is Lord. We have confessed that He always takes care of us. We have confessed that He has our ultimate good in mind. So let us remember these facts at our most stressful moments, most tempting moments and most painful moments, and confess our faith then, too.

We need to listen to our talk. When we hear words of compromise, or words of doubt, or words of mistrust, or words of judgment, or words of cursing coming out of our lips, then it is time to stop and repent. It is time to decide to believe God's promises and to speak them, and to ask forgiveness for our lack of faith.

To a large degree, faith is a decision. If we decide to speak faith, it will grow in our hearts. Our mouth and our hearts are tied together. Whatever we speak, we start believing. Whatever we believe, we start speaking. We can make a conscious choice. Joshua said, *"Choose for yourselves this day whom you will serve..."* (Joshua 24:15). We choose by deciding what we will believe and what we will confess. We choose by putting our words of faith into practice. We choose by repenting when it comes out differently than what we intended. We keep choosing Jesus until our talk and our hearts are congruent, saying the same thing all the time.

When the recording of my words is replayed at the judgment, I do not want to be ashamed. So I am starting today to watch all my words and to line them up with the gospel of Jesus Christ. You can do it, too! When our walk and our talk are congruent, we will be well on the way to maturity. Together, with His help, we will thereby make a positive impact for the kingdom of God.

Prayer

Father, I have a good confession in You. Help me to decide to always give it. I pray in Jesus' name. Amen.

Week 16

Faith and Hurry

For reading and meditation – John 11:1-44

"Yet when he heard that Lazarus was sick, he stayed where he was two more days." (v.6)

Everyone seems to be in a hurry these days. We have more time to do things, so we do more things. Our days get filled up. We overcommit. It is a mad rush all day long.

Jesus never seemed to be in a hurry to get anywhere. When he was twelve, He was not in a hurry to leave Jerusalem, causing his parents much concern. Later on in life, He was too late by four days to heal Lazarus before he died. That incident resulted in a resurrection. Another time, His disciples boarded the boat and set sail across the lake without Him. The result of that situation was walking on water. Out on the lake another time, He was in no hurry to wake from His nap, even though the boat was taking in water and was in real danger of capsizing. That episode resulted in His commanding the wind and waves to cease.

Jesus did not ever seem to be in a hurry. If you are in the center of God's will, there is no need to be in a hurry. God has orchestrated the events around you to fit His plan, not your plan. If we stay in tune with God and move in His will, there will never be a time we have to hurry. Jesus never hurried.

At the same time, Jesus was never late to do what God wanted. Sometimes it seemed from a human perspective that He was late, but He never was. If Jesus had sped things up and arrived at Lazarus's house earlier, before Lazarus died, He could have healed him. But Jesus healed all the time, and a more spectacular sign was God's plan in this instance. He could have boarded the boat with His disciples to be carried all the way across the lake, but it was God's plan to show the disciples a great sign.

Once when I was off to a late start, I hurried like crazy to arrive on time. I like to get places on time, but in this instance, I found that the start time had been delayed by the same amount of time that I saved by hurrying. God showed me that I did not need to hurry.

Perhaps one of the reasons that the priest and the temple assistant in the story of the good Samaritan did not help the robbery victim was that they were in a hurry and did not have time to stop and do good. It would have made them late. But what happens along the way is part of God's plan for you. They should have stopped. We should, too. The Bible says that if it is in our power to do good, and we do not do it, for us it is sin (James 4:17). Jesus was always being interrupted as He was headed somewhere. In each case, He took time out to care for those who caused the interruption. And God was glorified by it.

There needs to be balance as we consider faith and hurry. We cannot be so irresponsible that we are always late for

FAITH AND HURRY

everything. We need purpose in our walk. We are Christ's ambassadors on earth. We need to be going places and doing things, even though some of those things may seem quite mundane. In reality, they are the very things that God has ordained to change us to be like Jesus and to give us ministry for Him. Jesus was always heading somewhere to do something. He always got there on time, God's time, and fulfilled God's purpose for His being there.

By faith we can believe that God has also orchestrated all the circumstances in our lives. They are arranged in such a way that we do not need to hurry. If we continue to hurry anyway, He will put trials in our life to give us patience. Our patience will be exercised and we will slow down and live in more peace and rest.

Find God's purpose for your life. Walk in it. You will not have to run. If your intent is to walk with God's purpose, you can believe that all circumstances of your life have been designed with both your sanctification and your ministry in mind. There will be time for the interruptions as well as the planned events.

Maybe your life events need to be examined to see if they are all needful things in God's plan for you. If you can slow down, eliminate some of the extra and become a little more efficient, then maybe God will not have to orchestrate events to slow you down involuntarily. There is time to do everything that you really need to do. Go, do, and be all God intends for your life - by faith!

Prayer

Father, help me arrange my life so that I do not need to hurry all the time. I pray in Jesus' name. Amen.

Week 17
Faith and Streams of Living Water

For reading and meditation – John 7:37-39

"Whoever believes in me, as the Scripture has said, streams of living water will flow from within him." (v.38)

This verse is a test of faith, of belief. As Christians, we should expect to see streams of living water flowing from us. These rivers will result in fruit.

How can I know I truly believe in Jesus? The answer is in the verse quoted above. It is in the results that happen. Jesus said to the Pharisees who studied the scripture, that they did not believe the scripture or Moses, because Moses wrote of Jesus (see John 5:45-46 and Deuteronomy 18:15-19). It is possible to be a student of scripture without mixing that study with belief. We certainly need to study the scripture, but must always mix that study with belief and obedience.

Not only must we study and believe, but we must love Jesus with all our hearts. Jesus said, *"He who does not love me will not obey my teaching"* (John 14:24). If we do not love God, we

FAITH AND STREAMS OF LIVING WATER

will not obey Him, and if we do not obey Him, we are showing that we do not believe Him. If we do not obey Him, we will not even know His will (see John 8:31-32). It is important for us to obey all we know of God's will. This is how we show that we love Him and are committed to Him. If we combine our obedience with study of the scriptures, we are well on the way to believing what the scriptures have said.

When we believe in Jesus, there will be streams of living water flowing from us. Some effects of this stream may be visible, but others may be hidden from us. The reason some results of our belief in Jesus are hidden from us is so that we can continue to live by faith and not by sight (2 Corinthians 5:7). We need to continue to believe Isaiah 55:11, where it says, *"so is my word that goes out from my mouth: It will not return to me empty, but will accomplish what I desire and achieve the purpose for which I sent it."* Many times we do not know the effect of our words, prayers, or actions. We just need to believe that what we have done in faith will accomplish God's purposes.

True belief results in effects evident in the real world. In the book of Acts, one of the themes throughout is that signs followed the disciples. The gospel always went forth with signs; the gifts of the Spirit were manifested in power on a regular basis. People were healed, raised from the dead, bitten by snakes with no ill effect, delivered, saved, and filled with the Spirit. We can expect the same among believers today. Those with the Holy Spirit flowing from them in streams will be ministering to others in both natural and supernatural ways.

This stream of living water also results in changed character. This character change is from the inside out. It results in the fruit of the Spirit being manifested in every encounter and action. The believer begins to love what Jesus loves. Jesus loves people most. If the stream is flowing, we will be loving people.

LIVING BY FAITH

Jesus loves all of nature; He made it. If the stream is flowing, we will begin to love nature as well.

That God will pour through us His streams of living water is a huge promise. Yet Jesus promises it to all of us who believe on Him in accordance with the teachings of the Bible. Let us start believing in Jesus wholeheartedly in our thoughts, words, and deeds. Let us get those living waters flowing, and change the world for Him!

Prayer

Father, I believe; help me to obey. I want to see Your living water flow out from me to win the world for Jesus. In Jesus' name I pray. Amen.

Week 18

Second Chance Believing

For reading and meditation – Luke 1:5-24

"Zechariah asked the angel, 'How can I be sure of this? I am an old man and my wife is well along in years.'" (v.18)

The great saints of the Bible did not always believe God immediately. Even when visited by angels or spoken to in some miraculous way, they hesitated in belief.

Zechariah was an old man. It was his turn for duty in the holy place in the temple. Was he ever surprised when he saw an angel in there! The angel spoke and gave him a message. Just imagine: here is a fearsome angel standing in glory, giving you a message of things that seem impossible. What does Zechariah do? As if the angel standing there were not enough proof, he asks for a sign that these things that the angel said will happen. Not a good idea, Zechariah! We know the outcome: Zechariah was stricken with dumbness (he could not talk) for the next nine months, until his son, John the Baptist, was born. When an angel speaks to you in the holy place, believe him!

Gideon was even more reluctant to believe. An angel appeared to him (read Judges 6), and told him to go save Israel. Gideon also asked for a sign. In fact, he asked for a second sign after God answered the first one!

In both cases, God fulfilled His words to these men. He was bigger than their doubts and fears.

God will do the same for you. He will speak to you. He may not have an angel appear to you directly to deliver His message, but He promises in John 10 that you will hear His voice. If He has to use unusual means, such as an angel visitation, to get you to listen, then either the message is incredibly important, or you have not been hearing what He is already saying in other ways.

What if we doubt when God does speak to us? What if we should tell someone and we remain silent? Does that mean that God is limited or He will not do it? God is not limited. He will accomplish His word in you.

Even though they did not believe at first, each of these Bible characters had the attitude that they wanted to believe. One man, in talking to Jesus, said, *"I do believe; help me overcome my unbelief!"* (Mark 9:24). This is the attitude to have.

We are no better than Zechariah or Gideon. Sometimes we doubt, even when God speaks to us. Sometimes He urges us to do something and we resist. Sometimes He speaks to us in the scripture or a sermon and we go away and do nothing about it. God does not then give up on us.

He still wants to accomplish His will in us. We need to be able to overcome our unbelief. Perhaps asking for a sign is just what we need, to have our faith built up to believe. Zechariah had no doubts after the painful sign he received. After all his doubts in the beginning, Gideon was propelled on to great success. If it takes a sign, ask for it. God wants to build your faith

SECOND CHANCE BELIEVING

so that you will believe Him the first time. If it takes a sign, that is better than doing nothing. God is a God of second chances.

How much more do we like the stories of those who believed God the first time? Mary believed the first time the angel spoke to her. She responded, *"May it be to me as you have said"* (Luke 1:38). The shepherds believed the angels the first time by obeying their words and going up to Bethlehem to see the newborn Christ (Luke 2:16).

There is hope for us. If we believe the first time God speaks and act on it, great! But sometimes we fail to respond. Even then there is hope. God will still bring His word to pass for us. We need to call out to Him for help. Sometimes it takes a sign. Sometimes we just need to ask for help with our unbelief. He wants to help us believe. Then there will be another chance, and maybe another, if we need it. God is not going to give up on us. Let us keep pressing on toward the mark of obedience in fulfilling His will.

Prayer

Father, we want to believe and obey the first time we hear. But when we do not, we praise You that You are the God of second chances. Thank You in Jesus' name. Amen.

Week 19

Recognizing the Messiah

For reading and meditation - Luke 2:25-38

"Coming up to them at that very moment, she gave thanks to God and spoke about the child to all who were looking forward to the redemption of Jerusalem." (v.38)

It was easy for the shepherds in the Christmas story to recognize the Messiah. He was announced by angels. It is much more of a mystery how the wise men from the east recognized Him using their star watching, but they did. I do not expect that we will be given either of those two methods with which to recognize Him.

The part of the Christmas story that I find quite relevant in recognizing the Messiah is when Jesus is taken to the temple for consecration to the Lord as an infant. Two people there recognized him immediately: Simeon, a man righteous and devout, who was waiting for the Christ to appear, and Anna, a widow who worshipped at the temple night and day with fasting and prayer.

RECOGNIZING THE MESSIAH

These two people hold the key for us to recognize Jesus when He comes. We need to be living right, prayed up, and expecting Him to show up. Did you notice that when the Messiah came to them, He was disguised as a baby? No one told them to expect a baby.

He will also come to you in a disguise. If you are living right, prayed up, and expecting Him to show up, a disguise will not be an obstacle to you. You will recognize Him.

Matthew 25:1-13 is the story of the five wise and five foolish virgins. All were waiting for the bridegroom, but it was a long wait. When He finally showed up, only those with extra oil were able to enter. Sometimes we work up our enthusiasm and energy in order to be ready, but that is doing it in our own strength. In our own strength, we will always ultimately fail. We need God's strength. We need to be filled with His Spirit, the waters of life that never run dry. Then regardless of when He shows up, soon or late, we will be ready. Anna and Simeon did not recognize the Messiah in their own strength; it was because they learned to live in God's presence that they recognized Him.

When I was a little boy, I remember a book that my parents used to read to me called, "If Jesus came to my house." I remember it portraying all the good things that would be done for Jesus if He showed up. So when all the other people showed up throughout the day, they were sent away by the host, because he was waiting for Jesus. In the end we were told that each of the people sent away was Jesus. He was in disguise as just an ordinary person.

In another story, Jesus said, *"Whatever you did for one of the least of these brothers of mine, you did for me"* (Matthew 25:40). Jesus comes to us every day. Do we recognize Him? He comes disguised as someone that He loves who is in need, one of the

LIVING BY FAITH

"least of these."

We could respond coldly and say, "There is so much need. I cannot possibly meet it all or even make a small dent, even if I gave everything." If we do this, we miss the point. We were never intended to do it all. But we can do something. What is important is learning to recognize Jesus when He comes to you. Not every solicitation that comes your way is Jesus speaking to you. Not every good cause that comes to your attention for a donation is Jesus coming to you.

Jesus does come to you sometimes through those means. I think He mainly comes as the people you interact with and meet everyday. He comes with opportunities for you to do good, to help a fellow traveler have an easier time on the way through this life, or be directed to Him more perfectly. If you are in tune with God's Spirit by faith, as were Anna and Simeon, you will recognize Him!

Let us be continually filled with the Spirit. Let us be in prayer, living right, and expecting to meet Jesus. God will show up with opportunities every day for us to bless His people and, in so doing, to bless Him. Let us long to come to the point where we recognize Him every time by faith!

Prayer

Father, I want to recognize You every day. Help me to be ready. I pray in Jesus' name. Amen.

---— Week 20 ———

Faith and Peace

For reading and meditation - John 14:23-29

"Peace I leave with you; my peace I give you." (v.27)

Since Jesus came, there has never been peace on earth. Jesus said, *"You will hear of wars and rumors of wars… Nation will rise against nation, and kingdom against kingdom"* and *"…many will turn away from the faith…"* (Matthew 24:6-7, 10). Jesus predicted wars. There will always be a war somewhere, and rumors of wars other places. This will continue until Jesus returns in glory. Do not turn away from your faith because of war in the world.

In Luke 2:14, the first thing the angels said to the shepherds was, *"Glory to God in the highest, and on earth peace to men on whom his favor rests."* Too many times we only hear the first part of the verse: *"Glory to God in the highest and on earth peace…"*

Simon and Garfunkel sang a song called "Silent Night and the 7 o'clock news." In it, as "Silent Night" was being sung in the background, all the disasters of the world were being spoken in the foreground. Those who only hear the first part of the verse, like Simon and Garfunkel, will tend to reject the faith. Why? Because they say, "Where is the promised peace?"

The second part of the verse explains who gets the peace: *"men on whom his favor rests."* This is inner peace, not external peace. Read again Jesus' promise of peace in John 14:27, *"Peace I leave with you; my peace I give you. I do not give to you as the world gives..."* His peace is in our hearts by faith. Around us there can be turmoil. There can be overwhelming events. There can be war. But in the midst of it all, we who are in Christ can be perfectly at peace.

Jesus said, *"...in me you may have peace. In this world you will have trouble. But take heart! I have overcome the world"* (John 16:33). Our outward circumstances were never promised to be easy. It is our faith that makes the difference. We believe that Jesus has overcome the world. We believe that the things of the world are put here to test us, to build our faith, to draw us closer to Jesus. Therefore, we can rejoice in all our circumstances. We can live with the bedrock of His peace undergirding us.

The time in my life when I had the strongest sense of peace ever was when my outward circumstances looked the worst. I was lying paralyzed on a hospital bed in Manila, a victim of a rare disease. People would come in to visit, thinking I was dying, but I had so much peace, it was incredible. God healed me, but that is another story. There was a contrast between the outward circumstances and the inward reality.

The angels promised peace to those with whom God was well pleased. How do we get this peace? Be well pleasing to God. How do we please Him? Colossians 1:20 says that Jesus made peace through His blood shed on the cross for our sins.

FAITH AND PEACE

We become well pleasing to God by repenting and having our sins forgiven by faith in the work on the cross for us. First John 1:7 combined with Colossians 1:20 teaches us to continue to walk in the light if we want to continue to be well pleasing to God.

We can let our peace in Him be an indicator of how well we are doing. He promises inner peace to His people. We can live in this peace today and every day. We can expect stronger doses of inner peace when the outer circumstances get tougher. We never need to step out of His peace just because external circumstances seem to warrant it. That would be a serious mistake. Let His peace guide you. That is the true "peace on earth" that the angels were singing about. There will ultimately be external peace, but not until Jesus returns in power and the kingdom finally fills the earth. Let us make sure we are included in the people with whom God is well pleased, and receive the peace of Jesus constantly in our hearts.

Prayer

Father, I want to always live in Your peace. Let my faith remain strong in You regardless of my circumstances. I pray in Jesus' name. Amen.

Week 21

Sharing Your Faith

For reading and meditation – Daniel 4,5

Now I, Nebuchadnezzar, praise and exalt and glorify the King of heaven, because everything he does is right and all his ways are just. And those who walk in pride he is able to humble. (Daniel 4:37)

Daniel 4 is a letter that Nebuchadnezzar sent out to all the provinces in his kingdom explaining how he came to believe that God Almighty rules from heaven. This was Nebuchadnezzar's testimony sent to all the world. In it he shares his most humbling circumstances: the losing of his kingdom, and being made to eat grass like a cow for seven years. Finally, he shares how he prayed to God, was healed and restored.

I used to read this and say, "Cool, even tyrants can be saved." And so they can, and we should pray for them. But now I am encouraged to see a man who has come into faith and wants to share it with everyone.

Years later, when Nebuchadnezzar's son was king of Babylon, Nebuchadnezzar's testimony comes up again (Daniel 5).

Daniel tells the story of Nebuchadnezzar's humbling to Belshazzar. Belshazzar already knew the story, yet he never repented. Daniel then interprets the handwriting on the wall, a judgment against Belshazzar.

This comparison shows that we are responsible before God to listen to the testimonies of others. When we give our testimonies, those who hear them are responsible for their response also. If Belshazzar had paid attention to Nebuchadnezzar's testimony, he never would have been judged so harshly. He was judged because he knew what happened to his father, but ignored it.

Our testimonies are powerful. Revelation 12:11 says, *"They overcame him by the blood of the Lamb and by the word of their testimony."* We overcome Satan by the word of our testimony. We need to both have a testimony and to give it. Our testimony will overcome Satan.

Our religious discussions do not really have much power because we are speculating about some point rather than declaring the truth. Your testimony is your story of how God worked in your life. It is powerful. It cannot be refuted. Those who hear it are held accountable for it. It brings sinners to a point of decision: shall I believe or not?

Paul says to Timothy in II Timothy 4:2, *"...be prepared in season and out of season..."* He was talking about preaching the word, but there is an application for all of us. We need to be prepared to give our testimony at all times. You have a testimony of salvation, but you also have other testimonies of how God has worked. Pick the appropriate one for the circumstance, and give it. It is one of the best ways to start drawing people to Jesus. The devil is defeated by our testimony. Give it, using secular rather than religious language, so that your testimony sounds like normal conversation. Be sure to give God glory in your testimony; Nebuchadnezzar did!

Sometimes I wonder how I can witness to certain people. I pray in faith that God will show me a way, and He does. Many times He just makes a natural opening, and it becomes apparent that my testimony will fit right into the conversation. I can let the power of personal testimony make a difference, and I know that it will be heard. What I say will accomplish the task that God ordained for it. If we all pray that God will open a natural way for us to give our testimonies to some nonbelieving friend or family member, then God will hear us and open the way. Our testimonies will go out, and will work in people's lives.

Determine in your heart that you will testify at every appropriate opportunity, giving glory to God for what He has done for you. Do it regularly, do it often, do it with boldness! Then watch the forces of darkness get pushed back. Watch new people come to Jesus. It can happen through you!

Prayer

Father, give me boldness to speak my testimony in season and out of season. I pray in Jesus' name. Amen.

Week 22

The Goal of Our Faith

For reading and meditation – 1 Peter 1:3-9

"You are receiving the goal of your faith, the salvation of your souls." (v.9)

Salvation is both present and future. We look forward to salvation at the end of our time on earth, but by faith we are receiving it now. At present, our salvation is a continuing work. In the future, it will be finished. When we exercise faith, we are living in both realms at once, the future perfected state and the present fallen world. When we live by the Spirit and exercise the gifts of the Spirit we are partaking now of the things of eternity, our future.

Romans 1:17 says, *"For in the gospel a righteousness from God is revealed, a righteousness that is by faith from first to last, just as it is written: 'The righteous shall live by faith.'"* Martin Luther's great discovery was that we are saved by faith and not by works. It is our faith, not our keeping of the law, that saves us. It is the end of our faith that is the salvation of our souls. God does not weigh good works against bad works. If He did, we would be in real trouble. Thanks be to God, that He forgives our sin by His blood shed on the cross. We believe that by faith. We believe in His resurrection by faith. We receive His Holy Spirit by faith. We are changed within, receiving inner healing and sanctification by faith. We grow in Christ by faith. The entire Christian life is one of faith. *"Without faith it is impossible to please God"* (Hebrews 11:6).

This faith results in our salvation. However, faith has to be properly directed. You can have faith in the wrong things. Misdirected faith has led to the ruin of many. Remember that there is a battle in the heavens for the souls of men between the forces of darkness and the forces of light. The prizes in this battle are the souls of men and women. That is why we need to continually learn the ways of God. We need to become experts in the Holy Bible, applying by faith what we have learned. We need to listen to the Holy Spirit who has been residing in our hearts since we first believed. The Holy Spirit and the Bible will always agree. We need to daily remind ourselves of who we are, who we follow, and what we believe.

Our belief structure starts forming at a very young age, long before many of us were saved by believing in Jesus. We are saved because of the right things that we truly believe. We may still believe many wrong things, things contrary to scripture. Those wrong things that we believe will hold us back from the life in God that He wants for us. It is important for us to identify and renounce those false beliefs.

Faith is a gift. We need to ask Jesus to show us where we are weak in faith, and ask Him to remove the blinders and replace our misdirected faith and doubts with true faith. The more light that we have, the greater our belief in the things of the gospel, and the more God can use us.

THE GOAL OF OUR FAITH

There was a man in scripture who said, *"I do believe, help me overcome my unbelief!"* (Mark 9:24). That is a great prayer. There are times when we need to pray this way. For example: when we find ourselves doubting that God can use us; or we find ourselves lacking faith that God will meet our need; or we start doubting that God even cares about our situation. Then, because we asked, God will help us believe more perfectly. With faith comes change, but faith must come first.

Faith is necessary for initial salvation. Every step of the growth process in Christ is also a step of faith. Sometimes we are blind to our need for faith. Ask to have the blinders removed. Sometimes we want to believe, but just need Jesus to help us. As we grow, our faith increases, and we become more useful for the purposes of the kingdom. We are receiving salvation, the goal of our faith.

As we grow in faith we are being saved or sanctified. Do whatever it takes to get your faith to grow. Read the Bible. Spend more time with God. Sometimes counseling may help. It is definitely worthwhile to pursue growing up in God.

Prayer

Father, show me one of my unbelieving areas and help me overcome it. I pray in Jesus' name. Amen.

Week 23

Standing Firm in Your Faith

For reading and meditation – Galatians 5:1-26

"Stand firm, then, and do not let yourselves be burdened again by a yoke of slavery." (v.1)

How do we stand firm in the faith? Peter thought he could do it. In Mark 14:29, he declares, *"Even if all fall away, I will not."* We know the rest of the story. Peter denied Christ three times. He could not stand firm in his faith. The problem was that he was standing in his own strength. In our own strength, there will come times when we deny Christ, just like all the disciples did.

Jesus spoke to Peter later that night in the garden. He said, *"Watch and pray so that you will not fall into temptation. The spirit is willing, but the body is weak"* (Mark 14:38). In fact, He repeated this warning several times. If Peter had heeded Jesus' words rather than falling asleep, maybe he would have been given the strength to resist denying Jesus.

How many times do we resist the urge of the Spirit to watch

STANDING FIRM IN YOUR FAITH

and pray because we are tired and falling asleep? Certainly, we need sleep. Maybe it is a matter of priority. Watching and praying should be given quality time, rather than being carved out of our sleep schedule.

The words "stand firm" occur 11 times in the New Testament and 11 times in the Old Testament. For instance, in 2 Chronicles 20:17, the Lord says, *"You will not have to fight this battle. Take up your positions; stand firm and see the deliverance the Lord will give you..."* On the same night in the story about Peter, he took a sword and started to fight the battle. He cut off the ear of the high priest's servant. When we stand firm, we stand firm in faith. We do not usually have to do physical fighting, but instead, just watch God's deliverance.

We stand firm not by tightening our resolve. God actually takes part in helping us stand firm. *"Now it is God who makes both us and you stand firm in Christ"* (2 Corinthians 1:21). He is the one who has filled us with the Holy Spirit, the unchanging Spirit of God. As we lean on and trust in Him, we will be able to stand firm by faith: *"...it is by faith you stand firm"* (2 Corinthians 1:24). God helps us. Jesus prayed for Peter, *"that your faith may not fail"* (Luke 22:32). He also prays for us. It is not by our strength, but His, that we can stand. This is indeed good news. We are so fallible and weak, but He is strong, unchanging, and has made wonderful promises to us. He will never leave us or forsake us (Hebrews 13:5). He holds us so that nothing can truly harm us or remove us from Him (Romans 8:38-39). When we know and believe this, we can stand. *"Therefore, my dear brothers, stand firm. Let nothing move you. Always give yourselves fully to the work of the Lord, because you know that your labor in the Lord is not in vain"* (1 Corinthians 15:58).

There will be jostling and opposition in the faith, especially for those who are standing firm. The enemy does not like it. He tried to destroy Job. He will come against you as well. The ones who are standing the firmest make him the maddest because they are not letting anything move them. They are giving themselves fully to the work of the Lord. If you stand firm by faith, then you can concentrate on the work of the Lord, knowing that it will bear fruit. The storm around you will be gone tomorrow, but you will still be standing by faith. Proverbs 10:25 says, *"When the storm has swept by, the wicked are gone, but the righteous stand firm forever."*

That is the picture I want for my life. When the storm has passed by, I still want to be standing. I intend to let God do His work in me His way. I intend to let Him build faith in me, and I intend to exercise it. I intend to resist being intimidated by the storm, to just hang on tighter to Jesus when the wind gets stronger. It is in believing His promises by faith that I will be able to stand. You can do the same. He has promised to help you. Stand firm in the faith. Do not look to the right or left, but keep your eyes firmly fastened on Jesus, the author and finisher of your faith (Hebrews 12:2). Then when the storm has finished, you will still be standing victoriously in Jesus with the righteous. You can do it, by faith!

Prayer

Father, help me to believe in You so that no matter what kind of storm arises against me, I will continue to stand in You. I pray in Jesus' name. Amen.

Week 24

Full Assurance of Faith

For reading and meditation – Acts 2:22-36

"God has raised this Jesus to life, and we are all witnesses of the fact." (v.32)

Your faith is dependent on facts. It has anchors in real events that happened in history. 1 Corinthians 15:17 says, *"And if Christ has not been raised, your faith is futile; you are still in your sins."*

The central event of human history is the death, burial, and resurrection of Jesus the Christ. These are facts that need to be solidly etched into our belief system. If we do not believe that Jesus died for our sins and we do not believe that Jesus rose from the dead, then our Christian faith is worthless. Thomas said, *"Unless I see the nail marks in his hands and put my finger where the nails were, and put my hand into his side, I will not believe it"* (John 20:25). After showing him His hands and side, Jesus responds, *"Because you have seen me, you have believed; blessed are those who have not seen and yet have believed"* (v.29).

We are the blessed ones. We have not seen, but we believe. However, sometimes we still want some sort of sign from the Lord that He really did die for us and lives for us. In 1966, when I first discovered Intervarsity Christian Fellowship on my college campus, I saw, for the first time, a group of peers who believed. When they prayed, it was with the expectancy that Jesus was really listening and answering. When they read the Bible, they believed that God really spoke to them through it. I could see and feel their faith, and I wanted faith like that. So I started reading my Bible every day, something I had not ever done before. I also started praying this prayer: "Lord, I believe in You; make Yourself real to me." For six months I read the Bible and prayed that prayer every day.

Then, on an evening in March of 1967, God answered. He put faith in my heart, so I **knew** He lived there. It was finally no longer an academic exercise of wondering if I really had faith. I **knew** I had faith. I **knew** He was real. Romans 8:16 says, *"The Spirit himself testifies with our spirit that we are God's children."* It was a moment of assurance for me. I cannot remember a time when I did not believe about the death, burial, and resurrection of Christ. I always believed that Jesus died for my sins. The only problem was that I needed to **know** for sure. It was a real struggle, a real time of seeking, until true faith was found in me.

We can all believe in historical facts. We can decide to follow Jesus because of those facts. There is nothing wrong with that. Many people do. But I needed to come to absolute assurance in my heart that I was accepted by God.

There are many people who are now in the position I was in prior to my Romans 8:16 experience. They believe, but God is not real to them. There is no assurance in their hearts. You may be in that place. Perhaps you believe with a very shaky faith, not a solid, peaceful, and assured faith.

We are promised assurance. God has promised to make Himself real in our hearts. We can know in our inner being that we are saved, without wavering. It is worth the fight to seek God wholeheartedly until we come to this knowledge, which is the beginning of the true life of faith.

The historical facts of the gospel are true. We need to believe them in our hearts and not just our heads. To come to this kind of heart faith is a gift from God. Let us ask for this gift.

Prayer

Father, I believe in you. Make yourself real to me. I pray in Jesus' name. Amen.

Week 25

Foundations of Faith

For reading and meditation – 1 Corinthians 3:10-15

"...the fire will test the quality of each man's work." (v.13)

All of us are building a foundation for our lives. It is very important that we get the right kind of foundation. If the foundation is too weak, or is in the wrong place, it will fail when the test comes. Jesus said, *"Therefore everyone who hears these words of mine and puts them into practice is like a wise man who built his house on the rock. The rain came down, the streams rose, and the winds blew and beat against that house; yet it did not fall, because it had its foundation on the rock. But everyone who hears these words of mine and does not put them into practice is like a foolish man who built his house on sand. The rain came down, the streams rose, and the winds blew and beat against that house, and it fell with a great crash"* (Matthew 7:24- 27).

It is important to realize that both the wise man and the foolish man heard Jesus' words. We have all heard the word of God. God speaks in many different ways. In the passage quoted above, Jesus is speaking directly to the people in His most profound speech in the whole Bible, the Sermon on the Mount. If you have not read and studied Matthew chapters 5 through 7, please do so. Too many times we go away from hearing God's word thinking that it is enough to hear, but it is not. To only listen is to gain knowledge, and that is good, but knowledge by itself can make one proud.

Both the wise man and the foolish man knew the Bible. They could both recite the same passages from memory. They both had the same doctrines. They both went to the same fellowship. So, what was the difference between the wise man and the foolish man? The wise man put God's words into practice. The foolish man did not. That is the only difference. If we do not put those things we have heard from God into practice, then we are foolish. God's word will not do us any good unless we apply it to our lives.

We build a solid foundation by putting into practice the precepts of God's word that we have learned. Every time we put into practice a Biblical precept of faith, we are putting down another foundation stone. People who really believe will obey. If we say we have faith but do not have works, our faith is useless (see James 2:14-26). The Pharisees preached, but did not practice. Jesus warned against them. There are many people who call themselves Christians, and hold correct beliefs, but do not practice. They are on a very shaky or sandy foundation.

There will be storms in your life. It is guaranteed! The winds will blow against you. The rains of adversity will come. Your troubles will be unique to you, and they will be hard. Everything that can be shaken will be shaken. It is in adversity that the church grows the fastest. It is in adversity that the church becomes strongest. The storms in your life are designed to strengthen you.

LIVING BY FAITH

What an advantage to go into adversity with a proper foundation already laid! If we were already obeying when adversity struck, our behavior in the adversity would be to continue to trust God and His promises and live by faith. We would not only live through the storm, but we would not be harmed by it. Our faith would sustain us. The people living in the house on the rock did not have a care when the storm hit. Their house was solidly built.

If you just have knowledge of God, but have not been practicing the things that you know are true, it will go very differently for you when the big storm comes. The house on the sand washed away. It ended up a casualty, completely destroyed. There was not time to strengthen the foundation after the storm started.

The solution is obvious. Start practicing your faith now, while the river is flowing along smoothly within its banks. Become strong by exercising your faith before the battle. Then, when you get hit with everything all at once, you will be able to rejoice by faith in God's abundant provision. Build a firm foundation. Start today!

Prayer

Father, I want to be one who puts Your word into practice. Please show me how to lay one of those foundation stones today. I pray in Jesus' name. Amen.

Week 26

God's Armor

For reading and meditation – Ephesians 6:10-18

"Finally, be strong in the LORD and in his mighty power. Put on the full armor of God so that you can take your stand against the devil's schemes. For our struggle is not against flesh and blood, but against the rulers, against the authorities, against the powers of this dark world and against the spiritual forces of evil in the heavenly realms." (vs.10-12)

God's armor has a purpose. Although we do not see them, there are evil powers in this world. They strive to nullify anything you are doing for the kingdom by trying to divert you from the path God has for you. As you increase in effectiveness for the gospel, the forces of evil will come against you more strongly. You will have greater need to wear God's armor.

The devil's schemes are spiritual. His devices get you to turn your attention away from God, and to start trusting yourself or someone else. However, we have God's armor. The evil day will come, but with His armor we will stand our ground. We will not give up any ground, but, knowing the devil's schemes, we will even be able to take spiritual ground in the midst of the most difficult trial.

What is this armor? The first piece is **truth**. Truth is wrapped all around you like a belt. It holds you up. Get into the truth and get the truth into you. Jesus said, *"If you hold to my teaching, you are really my disciples. Then you will know the truth, and the truth will set you free"* (John 8:31-32). We get the truth by believing and obeying Jesus' teachings.

The second piece of armor is **righteousness**. The first time righteousness is mentioned in the Bible is Genesis 15:6, where it says, *"Abram believed the LORD, and he credited it to him as righteousness."* Our righteousness is by faith, by believing what God has said to us. Righteousness protects our heart like the Roman breastplate. As we continue to believe what God has said to us and continue to have His assurance in our hearts, we are protected in our most inward spiritual being.

The third piece of armor is **readiness**. We are called to be ready *"in season and out of season"* (2 Timothy 4:2). If two teams are equal in skill for the big game, the more prepared team has the advantage. If you are not ready, your defensive weapons will be overused before you ever draw an offensive weapon. The best defense is a good offense. Be ready with the gospel of peace all the time. Keep your walk true all the time, and you will be ready, as with a good pair of shoes.

The fourth piece of armor is **faith**. Faith protects you. It is by faith that you believe the truth about the gospel and about who you are in Christ. The fiery darts of the enemy are attacks on your faith. Hold up your faith as a shield and continue to believe, regardless of what is said or done to you. Let your faith deflect those attacks, so you can make your mark for the gospel.

The fifth piece of armor is **salvation**. Salvation is first mentioned in the Bible in the song of Moses, when the children of Israel crossed the Red sea, and Pharaoh's troops all drowned. The Israelites were freed from their bondage in Egypt. When we came to Christ, we were also freed from our bondage to sin. We continue to be freed as we press into Christ and our thinking aligns to God's point of view. God tunes our thoughts to His as we abide in Him. He puts a helmet on us to protect us from our old ways and thoughts, and to identify us as part of His army.

The sixth piece of armor is the **word of God**. This is our most powerful offensive weapon: *"For the word of God is living and active. Sharper than any double-edged sword, it penetrates even to dividing soul and spirit, joints and marrow. It judges the thoughts and attitudes of the heart"* (Hebrews 4:12). You need to become very familiar with what God has said. You need to know the word and be able to use it effectively. This is not just for a few (those called clergy); it is for all Christians, for anyone who wants to be in God's army. Every soldier needs a sword, and needs to know how to use it. Then the kingdom will move forward.

The seventh and final piece of armor is **prayer in the Spirit**. *"And pray in the Spirit on all occasions with all kinds of prayers and requests"* (Ephesians 6:18). *"This is the confidence we have in approaching God: that if we ask anything according to his will, he hears us. And if we know that he hears us—whatever we ask—we know that we have what we asked of him"* (1 John 5:14-15). Pray in tune with the Holy Spirit. Pray continually. It keeps the rest of the armor in place. Paul did not liken prayer to a piece of Roman armor, but it is just as essential as the rest.

So gird yourself with truth, righteousness, readiness, faith, salvation, the word of God, and prayer. If you do, you will

LIVING BY FAITH

certainly stand victorious, and even take ground when the battle is heavy. Being prepared is more than worthwhile, it is essential.

Prayer

Father, help me to remember to wear Your armor every day. I pray in Jesus' name. Amen.

Week 27

Faith Versus Sight

For reading and meditation – Hebrews 11:1- 16

"Now faith is being sure of what we hope for and certain of what we do not see." (v.1)

Faith and sight are two different things. If you see something, it is not faith. It did not take faith for Thomas to believe after he put his hand in Jesus' side and his fingers in the nail holes. He just saw! Faith is the evidence of things not seen. Jesus said it was better for those who never saw, but believed anyway (John 20:29). Faith is the certainty of what we do not see. We see it with our eye of faith.

Jesus will come on the clouds at the end of this age and every eye will see Him, and all the peoples of the earth will mourn because of Him (Revelation 1:7). This is a picture of sight, not faith. It will then be too late for any who have not yet developed their faith.

Some people are witnesses to miracles. In John 11, Lazarus was raised from the dead. In Acts 3, the lame man at the gate of the temple showed himself to all, walking and leaping and praising God. Although God may want to perform miracles for us, when He works mighty signs and wonders, it does not take as much faith to believe, because we are using sight. Remember, faith is different from sight.

The people in Nazareth, Jesus' home town, saw but did not believe. The children of Israel had the miracle of manna, and yet they grumbled. They saw it every day, but missed the fact that it was a miracle. What miracles do you see regularly that do not help you with faith?

Ironically, Jesus' miracles caused many of those without faith to be even more adamant against the faith. It does not seem like it would happen that way, but Jesus predicted that it would. When the move of the Spirit becomes more obvious, those who desire to live in faith will be drawn to it, but those who want to hang onto their sin will shrink more quickly into the darkness, plug up their ears and cover their eyes. The separation becomes more pronounced. They have to work hard at staying in the darkness, because Jesus said that when He is lifted up, He will draw all men to himself (John 12:32).

God says that our faith is precious. Faith, rightly directed, is what saves us. We decide to believe. When we believe, then God acts on our behalf. He honors our faith. He does good things for us. You can read about all those things in the Bible. Evidence piles up in our lives as a result of our believing, causing our faith to grow stronger. That evidence is still faith. We stake everything on a resurrection that we cannot really prove to anyone, on a future in heaven that we have not seen, on a Jesus whom most of us have not seen. We have the witness of His Spirit in our hearts. We pray, because we believe God hears and answers. We live righteously, because we believe God is watching and weighing our motives.

FAITH VERSUS SIGHT

Sometimes I think it would be great to be someone who sees visions and has heavenly revelations all the time. Then I think about what that would do to my faith. Too much sight, and I would not need as much faith. Remember, faith is precious.

Jesus was hesitant to show off His power. He did it primarily out of compassion. He wanted changed hearts. If God released too much power, everyone would have to believe because of sight. We are more blessed in believing without seeing the power. So do not envy those who have lots of "sight" experiences. They do not necessarily have it better.

Do you remember the story of the rich man and the beggar (Luke 16:19-31)? The rich man ended up in hell. He asked God to send someone back from the dead to warn his brothers. Surely they would believe if someone came back from the dead! But Jesus replied that they had Moses and the prophets. If they did not listen to them, they would not listen even if one came back from the dead (v.31). People will come to see the miracles, but will their hearts be changed? Will their faith grow?

It is those who already have faith that will have their faith bolstered by miracles. It takes a great deal of faith to believe for miracles. It is a stretching faith experience for those who would be used this way. But for the unbeliever, seeing will not increase faith. Let us not be like doubting Thomas who had to see to believe. Let us develop our faith without having to see.

Prayer

Father, help me to keep believing even though I do not see. I pray in Jesus' name. Amen.

Week 28

Trust and Obey

For reading and meditation – 1 Samuel 15:1-26

"Does the Lord delight in burnt offerings and sacrifices as much as in obeying the voice of the Lord? To obey is better than sacrifice, and to heed is better than the fat of rams." (v.22)

The old hymn "Trust and Obey" by J. H. Sammis is one of my favorites:

*Trust and obey, for there's no other way
To be happy in Jesus, but to trust and obey.*

We prove our trust, our faith, by our obedience. In 1 Samuel 15:22, Saul had just defeated the Amalekites, but had not done all that God had called him to do. To his excuse, Samuel replied, *"to obey is better than sacrifice."* Saul had done some of what the Lord called him to do, but had stopped short because of arrogance. He thought his way was better than God's way.

Often we act just like Saul did. We say, "God, show me Your will so that I can do it," when we really mean, "Show me Your will so I can decide if I want to do it." When God shows us His will, we are called to obey rather than to question. Saul questioned, and decided he knew better than God what to do. This proved very costly for him.

It is a good thing that God gives most of us second, third, fourth, or even seven hundredth chances to get it right. I can remember so many times when I felt the urging of the Lord to do something, and I resisted. For example, He would ask me to go up to someone and tell them about Him, or to speak out a prophetic word in a service. My thoughts would rise: "I will make a fool of myself. What if I do this and it is not from You, Lord? What will people think of me?" My hesitation would cost precious time, and then the opportunity would pass. I would then repent, asking the Lord to give me another chance, promising to do better.

The hesitancy did not go away easily; it was a battle. The flesh and the Spirit are at war in our members. God's explicit direction has not been given to me very often. When He does speak clearly, it is usually a challenge to my faith. We should commit ahead of time to obey God completely whenever He lays out an action for us.

We need to act on a directive word only a small percentage of the time. Most of the time our obedience is to learn the Bible, and align our lives to it. We stay in tune with the Spirit, keeping our lives pure and holy before the Lord. Then, when God speaks directly to us, we can hear and obey. For instance, when I was a university student in a large city, I used to go off campus to a large park to pray alone at night. One night, I had the distinct impression that I should not do it. I heeded God's voice, avoiding the possible danger that awaited me.

In the city of Damascus, Ananias received a revelation that he was supposed go and pray for Saul of Tarsus. Saul was known for tracking down and imprisoning Christians. Ananias had something to fear. He could have resisted God's direction, but he obeyed in faith (Acts 9:10-17).

If God tells you to do something, He is also asking you to trust Him. You must trust Him for the strength to do the task and that He will perform His part. Your faith will be stretched by what He requires of you. Do not expect it to be easy. You will be tested to the limits of your faith. God wants our faith in Him to grow. Consequently, He will always ask us things that stretch us. However big or small our faith is to start with, there is still room for tests of obedience. When we obey, our trust grows.

I believe that God funds His projects. He provided for me and my family to go to the Philippines for 15 years. When it came time for our daughter to go to South Africa for a few months, my faith was not big enough. I did not think God would raise all the money. God did not need my puny faith. I watched as she believed, and the money was raised. Watching others trust and obey can also increase our faith.

So let us obey God in all things. Then let us trust Him to take care of us when we obey. He will! Our joy will be full, and our faith will grow.

PRAYER

Father, help me to be quick to obey You fully when You call. I pray in Jesus' name. Amen.

Week 29

Seeking the Truth

For reading and meditation – John 14:1-14

"I am the way and the truth and the life. No one comes to the Father except through me." (v.6)

A movie entitled "The Gospel of John" uses a word-for-word rendering of that gospel. What stood out to me when I saw it was how many times Jesus said, *"I tell you the truth."* Jesus always told the truth, and He always did it openly. He went so far as to say He *was* the truth (John 14:6). Jesus is the truth, and He always speaks the truth.

Be a seeker of truth. There is truth about everything. To seek the truth is to seek God's perspective. To seek His perspective is to seek Him. He knows all things, all motivations, all hearts. He has the true answer for every situation. He knows just what I really need. He also knows what I want. He knows my shortcomings. He knows everything about me.

Truth by itself will drive people away. If Jesus knows everything about me, He also knows all about my sin, my failures, my rebellion, and everything else too ugly to mention. Jesus can know all of this and still accept me, because the truth is tempered by perfect love. *"But God demonstrates his own love for us in this: While we were still sinners, Christ died for us"* (Romans 5:8).

I can have faith in the Christ who knows everything only because He also loves me with perfect love. He will not gossip to others about my shortcomings. He took care of my sin at the cross, and will never bring it up again. He is looking toward the future, not the past.

Not only does Jesus know all about my past, He also knows about all the possibilities in my future. He has a plan for me and He knows the final outcome. It is His will to direct me in the path that will most conform me to His image (see Romans 8:29).

Jesus is totally trustworthy. Knowing that in Him is all truth about myself, and knowing that He completely accepts and loves me anyway, I can cast myself at His feet in abandonment with trust and faith. He wants to lead me into all truth.

Because Jesus always told the truth, I can also always tell the truth. I can tell the truth to myself and about myself. I do not have to hide anything, because I am accepted in Jesus. I can live free. That does not mean that I spread the truth about others' faults, because as Jesus tempered the truth in love, so must I.

Because Jesus has all truth, I can seek Him for that truth and expect answers. He said to the disciples in John 16:12, *"I have much more to say to you, more than you can now bear."* Maybe I am not ready for the truth that I seek. In that case, if I keep seeking, He will bring about those circumstances that will make me ready. He wants to guide us into all truth and actually promises to do just that: *"But when he, the Spirit of truth, comes,*

SEEKING THE TRUTH

he will guide you into all truth" (John 16:13).

Because Jesus is all truth, I can freely obey Him, without hesitation. He will only lead me in the way that is right. He will only lead me in a way that advances the kingdom. He will only lead me in a way that will more fully accomplish His will for my life.

Because Jesus is all truth, I have hope. I believe what He said about my eternal future. Death will just open the door to an inheritance worth waiting for in heaven.

Because Jesus is all truth, I can believe the entire Bible. He affirmed it to be true. I can study it and glean important truth from every part of it.

So rejoice with me that Jesus always told the truth and is the Truth. We can and will be set free from everything false because we are in Him. We can live our lives fully as He created us to do, without hiding, because we can trust the promises He made to us. We can stay childlike before Him, because he has tempered His truth with love.

Prayer

Father, make me a seeker after Your truth. I pray in Jesus' name. Amen.

Week 30

Jesus Came to Reveal the Father

For reading and meditation – John 5:19-23

"I tell you the truth, the Son can do nothing by himself; he can do only what he sees his Father doing, because whatever the Father does the Son also does." (v.19)

In the book of John, it is amazing how much Jesus talks about His Father and His relationship with Him. He came for the purpose of reconciling us to the Father. He wants us to have a love relationship with the Father. He wants us to worship the Father.

Jesus came to reveal the Father. In John 5:19 above, Jesus said that He only did what he saw the Father doing. He did everything He saw the Father doing. He is the exact likeness of the Father. He is one with the Father. There is perfect unity between Jesus and the Father.

As we grow closer to Jesus, we are also growing closer to the Father. Galatians 4:6 says, *"Because you are sons, God sent the Spirit of his Son into our hearts, the Spirit who calls out, 'Abba,*

JESUS CAME TO REVEAL THE FATHER

Father." "Abba" is the cry of a small child, the same as "Daddy!" in English. When we are born again, the Father truly becomes our father, and we can begin to relate to Him as a small child relates to his daddy. We are meant to have a relationship as familiar and as free as that of a small child with his or her loving daddy. A good daddy will always relate to his children at their level. Yet, there is never a question of who is in charge. That is how we should relate to our heavenly Father. He relates at our level, but He is the teacher. He is absolutely in charge, even though He wants to be familiar with us.

Everyone is formal with the president of a country, except for his family. We are the family of God. The Father is our father. The Son is our elder brother. We are family. We need not ever be formal with each other. Love relationships do not thrive if they are only formal. Formality may be acceptable in public, but real relationship must go deeper.

We live in a world where many people claim to know God the Father without knowing Jesus. This is the way it was in Jesus' time, and it has not changed. The Bible is very clear about this issue. We can only know the Father through the Son. The Son reveals the Father. Anyone who says he knows the Father in any other way is an impostor. It is impossible!

We need to look at Jesus. What did He do? What was He like? What motivated Him? What were His goals? How did He achieve them? This is how we get to know the Father, by becoming intimate with the Son, by letting the Son change us through the Holy Spirit.

In the world today, everyone is asking, "What are your goals? How do you achieve them?" I have a goal to get to know the Father. We can all have that goal. We need to find out what motivates the Father, take on His goals, do what He says, and live for Him. This calls for us to sacrifice not only our own goals, but even our lives. After all, Jesus did. Then we will truly be getting to know the Father.

We come to know the Father by faith. It is by faith that we believe Jesus is the perfect image of the Father. It is by faith that we risk following Jesus to attain a relationship with the Father. It is by faith that we lay down our ways and take on His ways. Then we start to become like the Father.

This quest is worth it. It is also totally impossible. It is only by faith that we can even hope to attain it. The Father has arranged all the help we need. But each step toward Him takes faith. It takes faith to believe for salvation, making us children of the Father. It is by faith that we received the Holy Spirit. It is by faith that we continue to grow. So let us continue on in faith until we cross the finish line, and finally are home with our heavenly family, in our Father's arms.

Prayer

Father, thank You for sending Jesus to show us the way. Help us to follow Him fully so that we can know You more intimately each day. I pray in Jesus' name. Amen.

Week 31

Faith and Communion

For reading and meditation – 1 Corinthians 11:17-33

"For anyone who eats and drinks without recognizing the body of the Lord eats and drinks judgment on himself." (v.29)

Communion is an act of faith. We all should be examining our faith when we take communion. It is a time to confess our faults, acknowledge Jesus as our savior, and recognize our brothers and sisters in Christ. All of this is done by faith. It strengthens our faith-bonds with God and with each other.

The children of Israel, on the night before fleeing Egypt, put blood on the top and sides of the doorframe (Exodus 12:7). Then they ate a hasty supper of unleavened bread and lamb. It was not the supper that saved them, but the blood. The lamb's blood is an Old Testament type of the shed blood of Jesus. Only those with the blood smeared on their doorframes partook of the supper. When God saw that they were under the blood, He passed over that household, not destroying the firstborn.

In 1 Corinthians 11 (above), Paul warns us that communion

is serious business. It does not save us, but it is open only to those in right standing with God. We are called to examine ourselves. Are we saved? Are we walking in faith? Have we confessed and repented of our known sins? If not, then it behooves us to stop and do so before proceeding.

Judas also took communion in the upper room on that night when Jesus and his disciples were celebrating the feast of Passover at the last supper. Immediately after sharing the bread with Jesus, Judas went out and betrayed him. Think of the terrible judgment that Judas suffered after eating unworthily.

We should also be aware of the meanings of the elements. Jesus first took the bread. This was on the eve of the crucifixion. He said, *"This is my body given for you; do this in remembrance of me"* (Luke 22:19). The next day, they were all to learn just what it meant for Jesus to give His body for them. He died for us. He took our sin on Himself and freely laid Himself down in an agonizing death, so that we could have relationship with the Father.

The Israelites were to eat every bit of the sacrificed lamb. Nothing was to be wasted. We are not to let Jesus' sacrifice go in vain. We are to partake of every bit of what Jesus has for us. Partake fully of Jesus. Decide in your heart to let Him do His complete work in you, and to follow Him fully with your life.

Secondly, Jesus took the cup. He said, *"This cup is the new covenant in my blood, which is poured out for you"* (Luke 22:20). This new covenant reminds me of a covenant that God made with Abram 2000 years earlier. The covenant with Abram also happened after communion. In Genesis 14, after Abram rescued Lot from Kedorlaomer, he met Melchizedek, priest of God and king of Salem, who offered him bread and wine. Soon after that, God made a covenant with Abram. Animals were sacrificed and Abram was given a vision of the future and a

FAITH AND COMMUNION

promise. God made declarations by blood and carried them out. It was by the shedding of blood that God declared absolutely what He would do. He could not and would not go back on His word.

In like manner, the new covenant is sealed by the blood of Christ shed on the cross. It is God's absolute promise to us that He will not ever forsake us, but will take us to eat with Him again in His Father's kingdom in heaven. It is symbolized in the drinking of the wine. When we drink communion, God again speaks to us and says, "Yes! I will do for you what I have promised. I will seat you at My banqueting hall in heaven at the great marriage supper of the lamb and you will sup with Me there." This will happen. Jesus will not break His promise. He sealed it with His own blood.

Finally, in 1 Corinthians 11, Paul urges us to wait for each other when we partake. The children of Israel had their Passover meal all on the same night. We are one body. There is only one body. Jesus' church needs to be in unity. We will be together forever. Let us come into unity now.

Examine yourself to make sure you are in the faith when you take communion. Remember how much Jesus did to win us to the Father. Decide to follow Him in every way. Remember the great promises that He left with us that He will fulfill for us when He comes. And be in unity with the rest of the body of Christ.

Prayer

Father, help us to always examine ourselves when we take communion. I pray in Jesus' name. Amen.

Week 32

Faith and Meeting Together

For reading and meditation - Hebrews 10:19-25

"Let us not give up meeting together, as some are in the habit of doing, but let us encourage one another--and all the more as you see the Day approaching." (v.25)

Meeting together as the local body of Christ is very important. We will have a hard time making it on our own. To put out a campfire, one of the first things you do is spread out the embers, so they cannot keep each other hot. That way it cools faster. Like that campfire, if we do not meet with likeminded people regularly, our fire for God will cool over time. It is not God's will for us to cool off. He will spit out the lukewarm (Revelation 3:16). He wants us to stay hot. The best way to stay fervent is to gather together on a regular basis.

Meeting together will also keep us on track with right doctrine. Ephesians 5:15-19 says, *"Be very careful, then, how you live—not as unwise but as wise, making the most of every opportunity, because the days are evil. Therefore do not be foolish, but understand what the* Lord's *will is. Do not get drunk on wine, which leads to debauchery. Instead, be filled with the Spirit. Speak to one another with psalms, hymns and spiritual songs. Sing and make music in your heart to the* Lord.*"* This passage asks us to understand the Lord's will. It is talking about how we live and about what to do when we meet together. The Lord's will is related to how we live. We can only understand the Lord's will by living it and obeying God. Otherwise, all we have is theory. We come to know sound doctrine experientially, as we hear it, believe it, and act on it. It takes all three for real growth to occur.

When the Bible says to spur one another on to good works, it really is talking about forming sound doctrine in our hearts. True doctrine is lived out. How do we spur one another on to good works? We do so by meeting together as a body, by testifying to what God is doing, by encouraging each other to do the right things, and by courageously standing up for Jesus wherever we are. We also encourage each other by prayer and ministry to each other's needs. When someone is having a hard time for any reason, he or she can be ministered to by the body, counseled by the body, and taught by the body. The ministries are there to meet the needs of the people.

After a time of mutual encouragement, we go back into everyday life. Every Christian is a minister. You have a ministry. There is a battle on for the souls of men. Those of us who are members of Christ are the soldiers in this battle. We need to pray for each other, knowing that there is a whole team behind us. It is easier if we meet together regularly to minister to each other.

It is also important that we receive sound doctrine so that our faith will not be in vain. After Paul received teaching from the Holy Spirit, he went to the elders in Jerusalem to make sure that what he learned was the same thing that the other apostles taught. Heresies have crept into the church because of lack of sound teaching. When we meet together regularly, we are opening our teaching to the scrutiny of others. This is good, as it keeps our doctrine sound.

We need to be filled with the Holy Spirit to truly understand doctrine. Doctrine is spiritual and is understood spiritually. We need to mix doctrine with faith, believing it and acting on it. Then we will know true doctrine, and we will grow.

It takes the anointing of the Holy Spirit to bring true doctrine to life. When I was young, I picked up the Bible to read and found it very dry. Years later, after being filled with the Spirit, I could feel its power as I read. Why? The Holy Spirit opened the eyes of my understanding to the truths of God.

Fellowship and ministry spur us on to understanding the scripture and acting upon it. Worship together opens our eyes to see and ears to hear what God is saying to us. We will feed our fires for the Lord when we are faithful in these disciplines.

Prayer

Father, help me to be faithful in meeting together with other believers, so I can stay on fire for You. I pray in Jesus' name. Amen.

Week 33

The Kingdom Within Us

For reading and meditation – Matthew 10:5-42

"As you go, preach this message: 'The kingdom of heaven is near.'" (v.7)

The kingdom of God is not yet a visible kingdom, but is only within us. Jesus said to Pilate in John 18:36, *"My kingdom is not of this world. If it were, my servants would fight..."* Jesus came to change hearts. He wants to replace our old hearts that are dead toward God with new pliable hearts that can be molded to His purposes. He wants us trained in all righteousness. He wants us filled to overflowing with the Holy Spirit. He wants our lights shining brightly before men. He wants us to be the "flavorers" of society, much like a little salt flavors the whole meal. He wants us red hot for Him. He wants us full of faith in Him, and what He can and will do. He wants us in constant communication with Him. In the kingdom of God, the citizens hear, love, and obey their king. The king gives them righteousness, peace, and joy in the Holy Spirit (Romans 14:17).

The kingdom may be hidden from this world, but you can observe who is in it. It is by their fruit that you will know them (Matthew 7:16). It is by the preaching of the gospel and the power of the gospel that you will know the kingdom is near. Everyone who comes near to it is affected. Isaiah 55:11 says, *"...my word that goes out from my mouth: It will not return to me empty, but will accomplish what I desire and achieve the purpose for which I sent it."* The only word that some people see is you. You carry the kingdom around with you. As you live in the Spirit, God is accomplishing His work through you. You may not even be aware of it. You are on a mission to be salt and light in the world. This is a matter of faith. Because God is accomplishing His work through you even when you do not know it, how much more important is it for you to stay close to Him, to avoid temptation, to listen to His voice and obey? Every word, every thought, every action can have an effect on the purposes of God.

Our battle is not physical, but spiritual. Being spiritual, it must be fought in the spiritual realm. The true enemies are principalities and powers in the heavenly realm that hold blindfolds over the eyes of humanity. These enemies need to be defeated. The coming of the kingdom defeats these enemies. People are never our true enemy. That is why Jesus said to love our enemies and do good to those who despitefully use us (Matthew 5:44).

People are bound by sin, deception, and other results of Adam's fall. The kingdom of God overcomes all of these: sin was defeated at the cross; deception is defeated when the gospel is preached and people believe; the results of the fall are defeated by the miraculous. All enemies will be totally defeated when Jesus returns and the kingdom comes visibly.

Everything God does on earth today is in partnership with

THE KINGDOM WITHIN US

the citizens of the kingdom. In Genesis, He gave man dominion over the earth. Satan usurped it, but God wants us to have it back. Consequently, He does not force everyone into submission. Rather, He gave us the commission to go into all the world and make disciples. When anyone enters the kingdom, it is because someone brought him the gospel, or someone prayed, or some member of the kingdom was a partner in some way for God to be able to reach that person. It is our responsibility to reach the world. All the power comes from God, but He will not act without us.

To be effective members of the kingdom, we have to be knowledgeable. We have to be disciples. It is not enough to just know and follow the most basic rudiments of the Christian message. Today the gospel has gone out to vast areas of the world, but the faith of many is too shallow. Making disciples means discipline, which means training, which means education. First, we need to educate ourselves. There is no excuse in our country for any member of the kingdom not to get an excellent training in Christ, as the resources are vast. It is your responsibility to learn and follow the scripture. Know what you believe, and why. Then you can be used to train others.

The ultimate goal is to make disciples of all nations. When that is accomplished, then Christ can return in power. Then the kingdom can come on earth as it is in heaven, as Jesus prayed in Matthew 6:10. Let us dedicate ourselves to that end. If we all do that, our generation will see the end of history as we know it. Let us take our responsibility as members of the kingdom seriously, living out God's will for our lives.

Prayer

Father, help me in turning all my time into productive time for the kingdom. I pray in Jesus' name. Amen.

Week 34

Faith and Giving

For reading and meditation – Luke 18:18-25

"How hard it is for the rich to enter the kingdom of God!" (v.24)

My faith is tested and built by my giving. It is harder to give when I have calculated just what we need, and there does not seem to be enough left over to give to God. That is the backwards reasoning I used while contemplating the purchase of a rental property. I was rearranging my finances to come up with the down payment. This meant taking some tax-deferred profits, all of which I needed for the down payment. The challenge was to tithe on the profit, and trust God for the down payment. If this real estate venture really was God's project, then He would provide for it. I went ahead and wrote out the tithe check. As I made the decision to do so, a great deal of joy flooded over my soul.

It is not easy to decide to give a tithe, but it is always the right decision. God has promised to provide. In fact, He once told me that there will always be enough money. I can trust

FAITH AND GIVING

Him enough to give a tenth of it back to Him. I prove my trust in Him by my giving. To a large degree, how much you trust in God will be reflected in your giving.

God certainly does not need our money. He owns the cattle on a thousand hills (Psalm 50:10). However, we need to give. The Bible says that giving is the way that we can actually test God: *"'Bring the whole tithe into the storehouse, that there may be food in my house. Test me in this,' says the LORD Almighty, 'and see if I will not throw open the floodgates of heaven and pour out so much blessing that you will not have room enough for it'"* (Malachi 3:10). God has plenty. When we give a tithe or more to Him, He promises that He will prove Himself to us in abundance. Take the Malachi 3:10 challenge, and test God.

It is a trap to refrain from giving because you cannot afford it. God's blessing is not released, you are short of money and cannot afford to give, becoming stuck in a rut. To release yourself, you must make the shift to giving the full tenth. It is at the tithe that the challenge in Malachi 3:10 starts. If you only give two percent and increase to five percent, that may be good, but it still is not at the beginning point for God's challenge. You could still be caught in the trap of lack. It is a matter of faith. God said it; I believe it; that settles it. Calculate your tithe today, and start giving at least that much. In the long run, you will really be glad you did.

The Lord loves a cheerful giver. It takes faith to give a lot cheerfully. Let the joy be your guide. When I decided to give the tithe on that large amount of extra cash, God gave me joy about it. He will do the same for you. You may be surprised by the joy He gives you as you decide to increase your giving.

In Genesis 2:15, God gave man the responsibility to take care of the earth. God has never taken that responsibility back, although the devil has tried to usurp it. God does His projects through us. Everything that happens for the gospel is accomplished through His people. We not only have the privilege of being part of financing God's projects, but we also have that responsibility. We need to put our money where it will do the most good for the kingdom. Therefore, I believe that we should actually give much more than a tithe. We are not tied to the law, but we are under grace. How much can you give cheerfully? What you do financially determines where your heart is. Jesus said to the rich man, *"Sell everything you have and give to the poor... Then come, follow me"* (Luke 18:22).

Riches can stand in the way between you and relationship with God. Those with an abundance of things are tempted to think they do not need God's help. It would be much better to see any abundance as an opportunity to make a difference for others in need.

Simplify your lifestyle, focus on advancing the kingdom with your money, and give cheerfully. You will find that you are giving much more than a tithe. You can finance ministries of various kinds all over the world, and still have plenty for your own needs. That is what I am finding in my life. It can be your testimony, too. Take up this challenge, by faith!

Prayer

Father, help me to trust You enough to give more. I pray in Jesus' name. Amen.

Week 35

Waiting on God

For reading and meditation – Isaiah 40:28-31

"But they that wait upon the Lord *shall renew their strength; they shall mount up with wings as eagles; they shall run, and not be weary, and they shall walk, and not faint."* (v.31 KJV)

We long to see God move. We want revival. We want miracles. We want God to break through to solve our problems. However, ministry may move very slowly. Perhaps we had expectations for this year that are not yet realized.

I went to a wedding where the bride and groom were both thirty-seven years old. It was the first marriage for each. The bride had received prophecy many times concerning her upcoming marriage, but she had had to wait a long time. In the same way, when God has spoken to you concerning anything good, you will be tested first. Will you continue to believe His word even in the midst of the opposite circumstance? The fulfillment will finally come. Sometimes we have to wait only a short time, but sometimes it is a long wait. For the believing

Israelites (Joshua and Caleb), it was still a forty-year wait to enter the promised land.

Waiting is like an airplane in a holding pattern. It continues to soar even as it waits to land. An eagle, while soaring, continues to gain strength and move higher. God may have us in a similar holding pattern. We can have the reward of the eagle in our wait. God is never late. He never forgets His people. He has His priorities right. We need to wait with perseverance, believing that God will both take us higher and do what He says. God is more interested in changing us into the image of Jesus than in solving what we think are our problems. He also wants us to participate in the deliverance of others.

It is not what we do for God that makes much difference; rather, it is how close we get to God by seeking Him. When our light is shining, people will come to it. We develop that light by spending time with God. Moses' face shone after much time with God (Exodus 34:29-35).

Before we are launched further in ministry or advanced in any way, God wants us closer to Him. We draw near by waiting. We wait on God by an act of our wills. We decide to focus on God. We read His word, we pray, we cry out to Him, we worship with our whole hearts. We listen to His voice. We persevere over time in His presence. It is not just waiting in the worldly sense, like waiting for the bus. No! Waiting on God is an active process that takes time.

Saul was a king who refused to wait. Samuel was late in coming, at least from Saul's perspective, so Saul offered the sacrifice himself (1 Samuel 13:8-13). Abram did not wait for the promised son, but produced one himself with Hagar (Genesis 16:1-2). Often, we are tempted to act before God's time. We need to be very careful. Our human effort will never produce the righteousness of God. In these two cases, disaster resulted.

WAITING ON GOD

We must wait. We cannot do anything on our own (see John 15:5). Let us wait for God to act, for God to provide, for whatever is necessary. He will act on our behalf. He will do it at the right time and He will use us as His vessels. It takes faith for us to wait.

By waiting, we increase our strength. We become more patient. We see the bigger picture. We persevere through trials and blessings. The waiting is not empty; it is filled with purpose. There is intimacy with God. We are built up and prepared for ministry. Waiting is not a bad thing. It is in God's plan for us.

Stop just sitting there. Focus on the Savior. Press in to know Him. Keep pressing in to know Him more. His depths are infinite. *"For the revelation awaits an appointed time; it speaks of the end and will not prove false. Though it linger, wait for it; it will certainly come and will not delay"* (Habakkuk 2:3). God will fulfill His plans for us. God will not disappoint us. *"For I know the plans I have for you,' declares the* Lord, *'plans to prosper you and not to harm you, plans to give you hope and a future'"* (Jeremiah 29:11).

So let us trust God with our future. Let us actively wait on Him and rejoice in Him in the midst of our daily life. In His good time we will see Him move in marvelous ways on our behalf.

Prayer

Father, help me to spend time waiting on You each day. I pray in Jesus' name. Amen.

Week 36

The Church

For reading and meditation – John 13:34-35

"A new command I give you: Love one another. As I have loved you, so you must love one another. By this all men will know you are my disciples, if you love one another."

After the Holy Spirit came, the people of God in Jerusalem started meeting together daily (Acts 2:42-47). They lived in community; they could not stay away from each other. They sold all their possessions and made sure the needs of everyone in the church were met. This type of activity went on for an entire generation. It ended when Jerusalem was destroyed by the Romans. Since that time, the church in its original fervor and love for each other has not been restored. Before Jesus returns, I believe that the church will again have the fervency of the first generation church. This restoration will happen all over the world, not just in a few small locations.

There is a bond in the Holy Spirit between believers. Meeting together regularly with the same believers over a protracted

THE CHURCH

period of time develops the deep relationships that God wants us to have. In Christ, our relationships can become much deeper than would be possible otherwise.

In the world today, people are running from one relationship to another, and running from one commitment to another. Because of a fallen nature, they cannot by themselves live the way God intended. When people get close to each other, they get hurt, problems develop, and there is pain. So they try to escape, instead of working through those issues as the Bible recommends. Proverbs 27:17 says, *"As iron sharpens iron, so one man sharpens another."*

Christians have a common goal: growing into the image of Christ. Rubbing up against each other has a positive effect, especially as we live for Christ and are guided by his word and the Holy Spirit. We *"spur one another on toward love and good deeds"* (Hebrews 10:24.) There is joy rather than sorrow.

From the very beginning, the local church has been a localized expression of a worldwide Church. The Church has diversified over time. When there are many local churches in an area, believers can choose a Christian mode of worship and belief that best matches their desires. Each local church contains people covenanted together to love each other. Each member needs to find a place to fit: a small group or a ministry within the church, or an outreach of the church. Frequent connections with other believers strengthen bonds within the local church.

We bond with a local church because of vital connection with people in it and with the God of it. Church membership more formally recognizes that bonding. It is a way of identifying ourselves with the God, people, and purposes of the local church. It says, "I want to be included in what goes on here. I want to have fellowship with you all. I have grown to love you and you have become as family to me." It also says, "I want to have input into your lives." Membership is two ways. Every member is a minister in some respect.

I have relationship with many Christians who do not attend my local church, as well as with those who do, and that is good. There is one body worldwide. At the same time, we need to identify with a local assembly that meets regularly, and whose people care about the state of our soul. We need to commit to an assembly where we get to know the pastor (or one of the pastors), and find ourselves truly cared for.

The true fervency of the restored church will happen in local churches and in the worldwide Church. To enter into this restoration, we will need to be well connected to our local church. At the same time, we need to have our eyes and ears open to what is going on globally. As more believers take up this stance, the church will increase in unity as Jesus prayed in John 17:11, 20-23.

Prayer

Father, I pray that You will open my eyes wider to what You are doing in my local church and in the Church around the world. Help me to connect better in both ways. I pray in Jesus' name. Amen.

Week 37

God's Plan for Us

For reading and meditation – Isaiah 55

"As the heavens are higher than the earth, so are my ways higher than your ways and my thoughts than your thoughts." (v.9)

Have you ever noticed that God does not always do things our way or according to our timetable? Sometimes we make plans and He changes them, or even totally destroys them. We can continue to trust Him anyway. God knows what He is doing. His main project is you, not your project. He wants to see the image of Jesus Christ in your entire personality.

There was a time in my life when I had my future all figured out. Then, in one week, I was fired from my job and had a large negative turn in my business venture. God had spoken to me in the past. He said such things as, "There will always be enough money," and "You are getting a spiritual promotion." The word of God is always tested. When someone prophesies over you, expect just the opposite to happen first.

Jesus' path was down, not up. He left heaven to become a

LIVING BY FAITH

lowly man, a created being. He suffered the worst kind of humiliation, resulting in death. After all that, He was exalted (see Philippians 2). This was a plan that no one could piece together as the path for the Messiah until after it happened.

God also has a plan for each of us. His plan may be one that is incomprehensible to us at this point. He is thinking about eternity and your eternal purpose. He is thinking about making you mature. He is thinking about the fruit that will come from your life when it is like Jesus' life.

Our way, like Jesus', may seem to be heading down. If we really want to know God, we need to let Him strip from us all the supports in our life other than Himself. We need to come to the end of ourselves.

If we go our own way, doing our own thing, God will interrupt us regularly to get our attention. These interruptions may come in the form of problems and trials. They will cause us to cry out to God, to submit our situations to Him. This is just what He wants. If we submit our plans in the first place, and wait for answers, approval, and alterations, then we may avoid a lot of the pain.

Expect God to alter your plans both as you submit them to Him, and as you are carrying them out. Expect God to take you on a route that requires you to develop your faith as you walk in His path. If you knew everything in advance, where would faith be? Faith is trusting Him for the outcome, not necessarily of your immediate plans, but of your whole life.

I can take the risky road rather than the safe road, because I know God is holding me. I can view my circumstances much like I view a game piece on a game board. Even though I know that God controls the throw of the dice, I will land on some good squares and some not-so-good squares. Every square has a perfect purpose, preparing me for eternity. Because He is the one changing me, I can trust Him and have a positive attitude in each circumstance, regardless of detours.

Remember Joseph? God had great things for him, but the route to get there was not the one he would have chosen. There would have been no exaltation without the severe trial. It may be the same for you. You can choose to rejoice in trials, in tribulations, in hard things. *"In all things God works for the good of those who love him"* (Romans 8:28), and you are one of those who love Him.

When God changes your plans, rejoice! You are then following a new path designed by Him and you are on the path to maturity.

Prayer

Father, I pray for the patience and faith to wait for Your plan for my life and then to follow it. I pray in Jesus' name. Amen.

Week 38

True Belief

For reading and meditation – Matthew 12:34-36

"For out of the overflow of the heart the mouth speaks." (v.34)

We behave according to how we believe. We speak according to how we believe. If you want to know what someone believes, then watch them and listen to them. They will give away their beliefs. If you want to know what you believe, then listen to your own talk. Listen to the scripts that run through your mind. Watch your own actions.

In modern society, we are sophisticated. The simplicity of having our "yes" be "yes" and our "no" be "no" somehow disappears. We attempt to hide our true feelings, convictions, and motives. We do this hiding in order not to hurt someone else's feelings, or so that what we say will be acceptable to others, or because we think the feelings we have are not acceptable. We hold high values for both truth and kindness and try to balance them. Even though we may be good at hiding our true beliefs, they will eventually come out in our words and actions.

After we have done some observations of ourselves and others, we will notice that our actions and words may not entirely line up with those of Jesus, or even those of His disciples. Being conformed to the image of the Son of God is a life-long process. If our actions and words are not lining up with those of Jesus, then we can conclude that our beliefs fall short of what they should be. Not our doctrines and creeds, but our beliefs, what we truly believe at a gut level, are what really count. It is by our words and actions that we can determine our true faith level.

Jesus said, *"If anyone chooses to do God's will, he will find out whether my teaching comes from God or whether I speak on my own"* (John 7:17). The implication of this verse is that we can only really know God's will by obeying Jesus and His teaching. If it is only in our head as a doctrine, but we do not put it into practice, we do not truly believe it. We truly believe only what we act on or would act on in the appropriate situation. Most of us have a head knowledge that outstrips our acted-out belief. It is easy to know right and wrong. It is much harder to always do right, even though we know it is right.

A big part of obedience comes down to counting the cost. The cost is high in terms of rejection by the world when we live for the gospel. If we always stand up for God and His truth, we will pay a price. Many have made a decision for Christ at one level, but have yet to even count the cost at another level. Consequently, we tend to do the things that are easier, rather than stepping out to do what obedience demands.

We need to resolve to follow Jesus – no matter what! No matter where His path leads, no matter what it entails, no matter how difficult or even impossible, follow Him one hundred percent. When God speaks to our hearts, when we learn a new truth, we need to resolve to put actions to our beliefs. Our actions will cause us to really believe. His yoke is easy and His burden is light (Matthew 11:30). We may pay a high price, but when we obey, we will find that the reward is worth it.

I was baptized in the Baptist church as a young teenager. I believed everything they taught me. I thought I was a Christian. Years later, after I knew I had encountered the living Christ, He convicted me of the need to be baptized again. I obeyed. I know it was the right thing to do, because I did it. Had I not done it, I would never have truly known if it were the right thing.

If you think God is telling you to do something, and it lines up with the Bible, then do it. You will know it was really God's will only in the obedience. There were times I felt God asking me to speak to a certain person, and I resisted. There were also times when I obeyed. I now know that I should not have resisted.

As we obey, we will grow in Christ. Our words and actions will start lining up more and more with His. Our light can continue to grow brighter, until we all are together forever.

Prayer

Father, help me to be obedient. I want my true beliefs to line up with Your word. Give me courage to obey. I pray in Jesus' name. Amen.

Week 39

Faith and Success

For reading and meditation – Matthew 6:28-34

"But seek first his kingdom and his righteousness, and all these things will be given to you as well." (v.33)

God wants us to succeed. He wants us to prosper financially, be in health, and have all our goals met. All of these things are good. But we can sit under "success" teaching without having true success. We can learn many of the principles of success without achieving true success. If the kingdom of God is advancing through you, or you are becoming more like Jesus, then you are achieving true success. Personal success, as described in the verse above, should just be a byproduct of seeking first His kingdom and righteousness.

It is true that God wants His children to succeed, but there is something that He wants even more. God's will for us is that we be completely conformed in character to the Lord Jesus. If there is no conflict between our character development and our success, then we will succeed.

There are real dangers in success. One danger is power. You are given power when you have a recognized position, some money, or responsibility of some kind. Everyone has some power. You have at least a little power. Jesus says, *"Whoever can be trusted with very little can also be trusted with much, and whoever is dishonest with very little will also be dishonest with much"* (Luke 16:10). We need to be completely faithful to God with the power that we have been given, even if it does not seem significant. Do not cheat, do not lie, do not steal. Repent when you have done wrong with your little power. Then you will be given more power.

A second danger in success is the trap of lust for material gain. In the parable of the sower, Jesus said, *"Other seed fell among thorns, which grew up with it and choked the plants"* (Luke 8:7). Later in the chapter, He explains this verse to His disciples by saying, *"The seed that fell among thorns stands for those who hear, but as they go on their way they are choked by life's worries, riches and pleasures, and they do not mature"* (Luke 8:14). In this case, it was success that was choking the spiritual life out of people. Life's riches and pleasures can choke your spiritual life. The American lifestyle is one of seeking riches and pleasures. Americans often equate riches, pleasures and material success with true success. This kind of thinking can choke out any spiritual fruit you may produce. Jesus thinks that spiritual fruit is more important.

The real issue in both these success problems is not the power, the riches or the pleasure. Instead, it is the direction or motivation of the heart. If the direction of your heart is toward the Lord in everything you do; if you want His will in everything; if you put Him first in every area of your life; then success will naturally follow. It is God's promise. If, on the other hand, you seek the success, you may achieve it, but like

FAITH AND SUCCESS

the children of Israel in the wilderness who asked for meat, you may also receive leanness of soul (see Psalm 106:15 KJV).

Therefore, it is far more important to work on living righteously, to spend time seeking God. Purify your motives in all you do. Examine yourself to see if you are remaining in the faith in all things. Then you will find your needs supplied. You will find yourself being promoted. You will be more successful than you ever dreamed. Along with that success will be a detachment from it, and a humility in knowing that it is God's gift to you for blessing others.

Prayer

Father, I want my heart to be right so that any success I attain can be used for advancing Your kingdom. I pray in Jesus' name. Amen.

Week 40

Rest

For reading and meditation – Hebrews 4:1-11

"There remains, then, a Sabbath-rest for the people of God; for anyone who enters God's rest also rests from his own work, just as God did from his." (vs.9-10)

One of the most overlooked aspects of our life in Christ is rest. Most of us do not get enough. Most of us just keep working regardless of how tired we become. My favorite verse on this topic is found in Matthew 11:28-30, where Jesus says, *"Come to me, all you who are weary and burdened, and I will give you rest. Take my yoke upon you and learn from me, for I am gentle and humble in heart, and you will find rest for your souls. For my yoke is easy and my burden is light."*

We can easily become burdened with many things. Life's problems and concerns can pile up. Relationships can tangle. Work can become too long or too hard or seemingly have little real value. This can all be very tiring, soul-tiring. It is especially true if we are not consciously in Jesus' presence while we are going through each day. We need to come to Jesus for His solution.

Coming to Jesus is not a one-time event. Rather, we need to constantly be coming to Jesus, bringing Him our thoughts, concerns and problems, and laying them at His feet. Then our souls have rest.

Next, Jesus asks us to take His yoke. Picture a pair of oxen tied together by a yoke, pulling a plow so that they pull as a team. Now picture Jesus as one of the oxen and yourself as other one. He is the bigger, stronger one, pulling the bulk of the load. His yoke would be too heavy for you to bear if He were not right there to bear it with you. The troubles and trials in our lives are too much for us. God designed it that way. There is only one solution. We need to yoke up with Jesus and let Him pull the load.

Jesus is not the easy way out of a difficult situation, He is the only way. The load is possible for us to pull because Jesus is bearing it with us. If we look for an easy way out without Jesus, our difficulties will just continue to multiply. We cannot get through them into real rest without Him.

Next, Jesus asks us to learn from Him. The learning takes place while we are yoked together. It is learning by example. If we maintain a constant awareness of Jesus, then He will speak to us in the midst of our circumstances. We can learn from Him as we go about our various tasks. If we remember to communicate with Him, we will find that He will give us insights. He is an expert in every field. Everything He tells us will prove to be Biblical. In teaching us, He helps us carry our end of the load better. In yoking with us, He carries the bulk of the load.

Jesus is not a hard taskmaster. Being gentle and humble in heart means that He understands our condition, our weaknesses, our faults. In fact, He understands them better than we do, and He does not condemn us for them. He does not fault us for not being able to do it on our own. He helps us. He teaches us. He forgives us. He takes us where we are and moves us forward with love and care, in gentleness and kindness.

We are called to stay close to Him, to let Him help us, to let Him teach us. He sees right through all our facades, our attempts to be independent or tough, and still loves us. We all need Jesus every day, every hour, every minute. Life is so much better when we are yoked with Him. So get yoked in and stay there. Let him pull the load and teach you how to pull your part better. All this is by faith. You will notice a difference!

Prayer

Father, I have pulled my own load long enough. I am yoking up with Jesus. Teach me. Bear my load. Give me your rest. Thank you, Lord. I pray in Jesus' name. Amen.

Week 41

Overcoming Evil

For reading and meditation – Romans 12: 9-21

"Do not be overcome by evil, but overcome evil with good." (v.21)

We are called to overcome. Jesus overcame the world (John 16:33). We can do the same by joining up with Him. Consider the battle that we each fight. We cannot use the enemy's weapons. He uses evil as a weapon. We cannot expect him to fight fair. He will lie, cheat, and steal. Because it is not fair, it may always seem like we are losing. Remember that it looked like Jesus lost when He died on the cross. Even though the enemy fights unfairly, we must overcome evil by doing good.

We cannot fight sin with sin. We fight sin with repentance. We fight lies with truth. As Christians we win by opposing the spirit of the world. We need to be born of God to overcome the world. 1 John 5:4 says, *"for everyone born of God overcomes the world. This is the victory that has overcome the world, even our faith."* Exercising our faith overcomes the world.

One day, I discovered a water leak at one of my rental

properties. There was nearly a foot of water under the building, and I could hear the rush of the leak. I crawled in, found the leak, turned off the water, rented a pump, and called a plumber. By day's end, all was fixed. The leak was an eighth of an inch hole in a copper pipe. It is amazing how a tiny hole like that can fill the whole crawl space with so much water. One small leak overcame the whole basement.

Sin can have the same effect on our lives. It only takes a small one, if allowed to continue, to undermine our whole life. Although we cannot keep the law, and are not called to do so, Jesus was adamant about the fact that breaking the law at any small part was breaking the whole thing. In the long run, a little sin can kill us just as dead as a big one.

Consequently, we need to examine ourselves. Are we walking in the truth, or have we compromised at some point? We can trust God to point out where we need to repent. He will find a way to get our attention. Our hearts always need to be made right with Him by obediently repenting every time we blow it. *"If we confess our sins, he is faithful and just and will forgive us our sins and purify us from all unrighteousness"* (1 John 1:9).

Every time we become aware of our sin, and turn back to God in repentance from the heart, we overcome the world. It is living by faith that makes us overcomers.

Revelation 12:11 says, *"They overcame him by the blood of the Lamb and by the word of their testimony; they did not love their lives so much as to shrink from death."* When we believe that Jesus died and shed His blood on the cross for us, and identify with Him in submission to His will, then we are overcomers. The world cannot hurt us any more. We are trusting Jesus to take care of our every need. Our circumstances are submitted to His control. We can do what is right in every situation, because it is Jesus we desire to please, and not ourselves.

We also overcome by our words. When we give praise to God in our circumstances, we are testifying. He is in control, so we can give Him glory verbally, with explanations in the hearing of those not yet born again. This is overcoming by the word of our testimony.

It is all by faith. We identify with Christ by faith. We trust Him by faith. We testify by faith. We overcome by faith. Jesus promised that we are to be overcomers, so let us start living it out today!

Prayer

Father, reveal to me where I need to change today to become a more obedient overcomer. I pray this in Jesus' name. Amen.

Week 42

Faith Leads to the Cross

For reading and meditation – Matthew 27:32-50

"As they were going out, they met a man from Cyrene, named Simon, and they forced him to carry the cross." (v.32)

Jesus first mentioned the cross in Matthew 10:38-39 when He said, *"Anyone who does not take his cross and follow me is not worthy of me. Whoever finds his life will lose it, and whoever loses his life for my sake will find it."* At this point, no one knew that Jesus was headed to die on a Roman cross. Romans were in control of the country and everyone knew that crucifixion was the Romans' way of dealing with troublemakers. Taking up a cross always meant humiliation, torture, and death. So why would Jesus tell us to take our cross and follow Him?

Jesus knew He was headed to the cross. If we choose to follow Jesus with our whole hearts, then we will need to die to ourselves and offer up our own aspirations in life. If we choose to follow Jesus, we need to lay down our own pursuits; we need to lose our own life. Jesus says that if we do not put Him first,

FAITH LEADS TO THE CROSS

we are not worthy of Him.

Too many Christians want to live in the best of both worlds. We want our own life, and His, too. Jesus says that this cannot be done. Some of my friends embarked on the road to heaven. They accepted Jesus, received forgiveness for their sins, and started on the road to life. But along the way something happened. A choice was made. They decided that they needed to find themselves, and, ever since, they have been pursuing their own lives. Christ's call has been ignored.

We are faced with some aspect of this choice every day. Will we pursue our own priorities, or will we pursue His priorities? *"Whoever finds his life will lose it, and whoever loses his life for my sake will find it"* (Matthew 10:39). Every day we need to give all we have to Him. We need to relentlessly pursue Him. We need to take up our cross and follow every day. This is a primary commitment that we must make.

Secondly, we need to know that God is not a hard taskmaster. He is a loving God. He wants the best for us. His will for us is what we were made for. His path of taking up the cross actually leads to life, resurrection life, more joy than we can imagine, forever. He will incorporate our gifts and talents. He will put us in a place where we fit, a place we will not find if we try to find that place by ourselves.

Before I went to the Philippines, or even knew I was going to go, I was prophesied over. God said He had a job for me. I had been praying to be used and to be sent, and He took me at my word and sent me, giving me the best job I ever had. It fit me perfectly.

He never promised that taking up the cross would be easy. Everything in the old nature says to run from that, to find your own life. It is only by faith and trust in Him that we can continue on course. It is only by faith that we can take up the cross

LIVING BY FAITH

and walk in humility, knowing that there will be persecution and hardship.

We are called to lose our lives for His sake. We can do this by identification with Him. Galatians 2:20 says, *"I have been crucified with Christ and I no longer live, but Christ lives in me. The life I live in the body, I live by faith in the Son of God, who loved me and gave himself for me."*

By faith, take up your cross and follow Him. Identify with His death. Ask the hard things of Him. Ask Him to use you, to send you, to prepare you for His service. Then expect an answer. He has a plan. He has a purpose. He will prepare you. He will send you. It will be more than just worth it, it will be glorious! Set your course today. Take the high road to the cross, taking up His way, not your own. Come and die – and truly live. Go His way – finding your true way. Start today by faith.

Prayer

Father, help me to make the commitment to take up my cross and follow Jesus every day. I pray in Jesus' name. Amen.

Week 43

Sowing Seed by Faith

For reading and meditation – Genesis 1:11-30

"The land produced vegetation: plants bearing seed according to their kinds and trees bearing fruit with seed in it according to their kinds. And God saw that it was good." (v.12) *"Then God said, 'I give you every seed-bearing plant on the face of the whole earth and every tree that has fruit with seed in it. They will be yours for food.'"* (v.29)

God initiated the physical law of sowing and reaping in Genesis. Seeds produce after their own kind. In order to get tomatoes, you have to plant tomato seeds. In like manner, if you sow financially, you will reap financially. If you plant seeds of kindness, you will receive kindness. If you are a friend, you will have friends. If you sow love, you will reap love.

On the other hand, if you do not sow these things, you cannot expect to reap them. It will be a surprise if you do, as they could have been sown some other way. Sometimes tomato plants spring up just because a tomato is left unpicked from the year before. In like manner, some of your acts of kindness from the past may yet bear fruit.

This law also applies for the sowing of hate or anger or bitterness. They also produce harvests, harvests that you do not want. That is why in Leviticus 19:19 it says, *"Do not plant your field with two kinds of seed."* Our vegetable garden has different kinds of seeds in it, producing a different crop in each row. This verse, however, has a spiritual application. We can plant seeds from the new nature or we can plant seeds from the old nature. If we plant both ways, we send a mixed signal and our fruit becomes ineffective.

When we live a life in the Spirit, we produce the fruit of the Spirit. Galatians 5:22-23 says, *"But the fruit of the Spirit is love, joy, peace, patience, kindness, goodness, faithfulness, gentleness and self-control."* Within each piece of fruit are seeds. When we produce the fruit of the Spirit, we are scattering seeds of the Spirit. We become a sower in our world of the seeds of the Spirit. This happens regardless of whether or not we are aware of our activity of sowing seed. On the other hand, if we are living a life following the sinful nature, we are producing fruit of that life and are scattering seeds of death to our world instead of seeds of life.

Jesus promises that the seeds we sow will produce a crop. Which kind will we scatter? We cannot help but scatter seeds. What we truly believe, we will live out. The seeds of what we believe will be distributed to others. We have an impact on people around us, even if we do not see it.

I encourage using your words to bring witness to people. However, your actions speak much louder. If you really are living in the Spirit, people will notice as the fruits of the Spirit become evident. Those seeds will be planted in them. Then your words will have a much more powerful effect. If your life does not look any different from the average person on the street, the effect of your words will be much less. After all, words are also seeds. What comes out of your mouth is what is in your heart. Those words produce a crop and spread seeds to others.

In the parable of the sower in Matthew 13, the sower sows seed indiscriminately on the field. We are sowers who are sowing indiscriminately on our field. Our field is everywhere we are, everyone we are around. We are sowing seeds of some kind into each of them. That is one of our callings, just to sow seed.

We can increase the quality of our seed by spending time every day in the Bible and in communion with Jesus. We can expand the quantity of our seed by being more involved with others. After all, it is hard to sow seed if you do not go out to the field. We may not see the harvest that will develop from the seed we sow, but it certainly will come. Believe it, and sow spiritual seed every day with faith for a good harvest.

Prayer

Father, help me to be aware of my sowing. May I always sow seeds of the Spirit and not of the flesh. I pray in Jesus' name. Amen.

Week 44

Faith and the Desert

For reading and meditation – Matthew 4:1-11

"Then Jesus was led by the Spirit into the desert to be tempted by the devil." (v.1)

The desert is barren, deserted, usually too hot or too cold, dry and quite rugged in terrain. It is a place to pass through, not to live. I like to head out to the wilderness for a day-long hike, but it is nice to be home again at the end of the day. The elements necessary for life are sparse in the desert.

Another kind of wilderness in which we might find ourselves is a spiritual one. Life does not seem to be heading in the direction we want it to be going, and we do not know which way to turn. Perhaps we had prophecy over us, and precious promises from the word spoken to us, but nothing seems to be happening now. Every way we try to go is a dead end. Prayer just seems to bounce off the heavens. What happened to that joyous experience of salvation? If you can identify with this sort of description, then you are having a wilderness experience.

FAITH AND THE DESERT

The first thing is to realize why we are in the wilderness. Jesus went to the wilderness to be tempted of the devil. In James 1:2-4 it says, *"Consider it pure joy, my brothers, whenever you face trials of many kinds, because you know that the testing of your faith develops perseverance. Perseverance must finish its work so that you may be mature and complete, not lacking anything."* We are in the wilderness for a time of testing. Temptations arise. We resist, or we give in. God reveals what work still needs doing in us to make us perfect. Our faith is tried to the limit. We should rejoice in this experience because God changes us through it. Sometimes, even when we fail the test, we learn the lesson and are able to move forward.

There are definite reasons for the wilderness. We need to learn the lessons best taught there in order to move on into the calling God has for us. Jesus was tempted three times in the wilderness. He passed His test and moved on. The children of Israel who followed Moses around the wilderness for forty years had ten tests, and failed most of them. The Israelites were miraculously given manna to eat while they were in the wilderness. They complained about it. They complained about lack of water. We will certainly be tested in the wilderness. Will we pass and be able to move on, or fail and need to take another lap? Most of these people never left the wilderness. So how do we get out of the wilderness?

Your tests will be specifically tailored to you. You have a distinct personality. You are vulnerable in certain areas. The tests that others fail may be easy for you to pass, and vice versa. God knows what He is doing.

So persevere. Recognize the wilderness. Decide to make it through. There will be no shortcuts. Shortcuts are usually failed tests. The Israelites received quail in the wilderness when they complained to God about the lack of meat to eat (Numbers

11:4-14, 31-34), but along with it came much distress. Jesus was offered a shortcut to world dominion by the devil when He was in the wilderness (Matthew 4:9-10). He successfully resisted by properly using the scripture.

We need to realize that our tests are not too hard for us. God never allows us to be tempted above what He can enable us to resist. We can be successful in our wilderness. It will take patience. It will take reliance on the scripture. It will take seeking God with all our hearts. But in the end, it will be worth it. The struggle that we have in the wilderness will make us strong and able to meet the challenges to come.

So do not give up. Press through. Every wilderness has an end. Jesus was there 40 days. Some are there much longer, but there is a time that the wilderness will end. The lessons learned there will be part of your strength. Remember to rejoice in the midst of your desert. You will then be prepared for a new level of ministry.

Prayer

Father, I thank you for the wilderness. Help me to persevere through my wilderness experience until I can exit with lessons learned. I pray in Jesus' name. Amen.

Week 45

Following Jesus

For reading and meditation – Mark 2:1-14

"'Follow me,' Jesus told him, and Levi got up and followed him."
(v.14)

What does it mean to be a follower? The apostle Paul said, *"Whatever you have learned or received or heard from me, or seen in me—put it into practice. And the God of peace will be with you"* (Philippians 4:9). In at least twenty places in the New Testament, Jesus said, *"Follow me."*

Following Jesus involves at least two things. First, we need to do what He says. Second, we need to do what He does. If all God needed to do was tell us things, or tell us how to live, He could have done that without sending His Son. But God does not just speak. He demonstrates; He acts out how to live. Do not get me wrong; we need all of Jesus' teaching, like the sermon on the mount and all the parables. We should pay attention to every word. Too much of the time we only pay attention to what Jesus said, and neglect paying attention to how

He lived. We have Bibles with red print for all of Jesus' words. Perhaps we need another color to note all of Jesus' actions.

If we pay attention to how Jesus lived, we will gain great insights into how we should be ordering and disciplining our lives. Some of the ways that Jesus lived can only be figured out by clues. For instance, in the wilderness (Matthew 4), Jesus used scripture to defeat the devil. He was a student of the scripture. He knew what it meant, and He knew how to use it. We, as followers, should also discipline ourselves to know and use the scriptures.

From this same passage, there are other insights we can derive about how Jesus lived. He fasted. As His followers, we should also fast. He spent extended time alone with God. That happened not only in the wilderness, but also in many other places. Often we are content to give God just a few minutes; we are content with one meal from God. There is nothing wrong with this, but we also need provision in our life for extended time alone with Him. How often have you read an entire Gospel through in one sitting? From this one little glimpse of Jesus, we see the discipline of learning the Bible, fasting, and spending extended time alone with God.

If we pay attention to how Jesus lived, we will see the results of a Spirit-led life. Jesus was certainly Spirit-led in everything. One result was perfect peace in the midst of the storm (Matthew 8:23-26). If we are living in the center of God's will, being led by the Spirit, we will have perfect peace regardless of the storm raging around us and threatening to overcome us.

If we pay attention to the way Jesus lived, we will notice He mixed with sinners, not just saints. Matthew 9:10 says, *"many tax collectors and 'sinners' came and ate with him and his disciples."* Do sinners come and eat with you? If we are following Jesus, we should invite those from outside the family of believers to eat at our house. How else are they going to be won?

Jesus was able to be interrupted. He was not so engrossed in any task that He could not stop what He was doing to help someone in need. There are many examples of this. In fact, most of His ministry seems to be one of interruption. Are we open to interruptions in our lives? God puts them there as opportunities. We can walk by on the other side and continue with our plan, or disrupt our plan and do something that will probably make a real difference for someone. That seems to be what Jesus always did. He not only told the story of the good Samaritan, but He acted it out several times.

My own record is much worse. Yes, I have allowed myself to be interrupted on occasion, but there are too many times when I decided not to get involved. To follow Jesus, we need to get involved with the opportunities before us to do someone good, especially when there is no one else to help.

To be a follower of Jesus, we need to read our Bibles with a new interest. Look for what Jesus did, then ask the question, "How can I apply that to my life?" Remember, it is not knowledge alone, but application of that knowledge that makes a difference. We can trust Jesus to change us on the inside to love others like He does. Become a follower of Christ in word and in deed. Your faith will grow. You will become stronger in Him!

Prayer

Father, I want to be a follower of Jesus in word and in deed. Show me how, as I study the scripture and spend time with You. In Jesus' name I pray. Amen.

Week 46

Faith and Failure

For reading and meditation – 1 Corinthians 4:10-16

"When we are cursed, we bless; when we are persecuted, we endure it; when we are slandered, we answer kindly. Up to this moment we have become the scum of the earth, the refuse of the world." (vs.12-13)

From a worldly point of view, Paul was a failure. He was beaten, imprisoned, rejected, driven out of town. He experienced many other abuses, and was treated as a criminal. Yet he says, "Imitate me" (1 Corinthians 4:16). Jesus was despised and rejected, dying as a criminal on a Roman cross, a failure by any worldly standard. His disciples were also martyred for their faith.

Likewise, we will be hated by the world, because the world hates Jesus and His message. Today, there are more active Christians in the underground church in China than there are active Christians in the church in the United States. For those Chinese Christians, worldly failure is expected. To be found

FAITH AND FAILURE

out means only the most menial job will be allotted. They will not be allowed to succeed by any worldly standard: finances or position or the possibility of taking a vacation. Many will be harassed by police, some arrested, and a few even killed. To become a Christian in China is to realize that this type of persecution awaits. In some other countries it is even worse. Yet people are willing to make that sacrifice, and the church continues to grow.

In this "Christianized" United States, rejection is more subtle. If we commit ourselves to speaking up whenever the Holy Spirit prompts us, if we stand up for the gospel and the teachings of the gospel in our society, the enemies of the cross will not be as violent in their rejection of us. They may even do it politely. But they will still reject us. They will exclude us and attempt to marginalize us. It will feel like failure.

This kind of failure is all good news. Failure is part of being on the right path. Jesus said that if they reject Him, they will reject us (see John 15:20). When we are rejected for the gospel, we should rejoice. Jesus said, *"Blessed are you when people insult you, persecute you and falsely say all kinds of evil against you because of me. Rejoice and be glad, because great is your reward in heaven, for in the same way they persecuted the prophets who were before you"* (Matthew 5:11-12).

The danger comes when we are never rejected for the gospel. When we are always accepted, we should consider it a warning. It may be a sign that we are compromising the gospel, that our witness is not effective, or that we are not bearing fruit. John Wesley, the 18th century founder of Methodism, thought of his preaching as a failure if he did not encounter some opposition and rejection every time he preached.

Too often we realize that there will be rejection if we speak up for Jesus in our circle, so we refrain from doing it. It is more important for us to be accepted than it is for us to spread the good news. If that is your attitude, repent. Examine yourself on this point. Do you compromise your witness to avoid rejection? Or do you let who you are in Christ just shine through without compromise? If you are compromising, you are not experiencing any rejection. If you let Jesus shine through, you will experience some rejection, be it ever so subtle.

Experiencing that rejection is part of Jesus' plan for us. We need to expect it. It will make us strong. We will be able to stand up for Him more strongly when the heavier persecution starts happening. Heavier persecution will start happening at some point. You will not be ready for it unless you let Jesus' program of failure do its work in you now.

There is spiritual warfare going on right now. The outcome of this battle is in the hands of God's people. Will we humble ourselves enough to experience the rejection of the world? Decide today to let your light shine in your world all the time regardless of the outcome. Rejoice when rejection comes, and move on. It is all part of the plan.

Prayer

Father, give me courage to stand for You in every situation. I pray in Jesus' name. Amen.

Week 47

Loving Our Neighbor

For reading and meditation – Luke 16:19-31

"But Abraham replied, 'Son, remember that in your lifetime you received your good things, while Lazarus received bad things, but now he is comforted here and you are in agony.'" (v.25)

In this story, the rich man was given the opportunity to help a poor beggar. The beggar was at his gate every day, yet he was ignored. The rich man may have been a leader in the community. He may have thought that riches were a reward for being good. But God was more interested in what he did to help his fellow man who was struggling. Proverbs 3:27-28 says, *"Do not withhold good from those who deserve it, when it is in your power to act. Do not say to your neighbor, 'Come back later; I'll give it tomorrow' – when you now have it with you."*

It was in the rich man's power to help Lazarus. He could have tended to his sores but did not, since we know that the dogs licked them. He could have fed him. We do not know whether he did anything for the beggar, but we do know that he could have done much more.

When poverty is everywhere, it is difficult to know what to do. We cannot help everyone, and if we try helping a few, many more will soon show up. We are only called to do what we can do with Jesus' help. We are only called to help those placed before us. We must at least do something to help.

In Jesus' story, Lazarus, the needy one, showed up on the rich man's doorstep. This was a test for the rich man. We all have tests of faith to pass. Could he humble himself enough to love his neighbor? It was painfully obvious what he needed to do, yet he did not do it.

Today, the world has shrunk. The needy ones may not be on our doorstep. Most of them may be on the other side of the world. But it is still in our power to help them. Of course, we cannot help them all, but there are programs by which we can help an individual orphan in need, for instance. For a small amount per day the life of an orphan overseas can be rescued now and for all eternity. Our doorstep has enlarged since the days of Lazarus and the rich man.

Most of us are the rich men. In this story, the rich man ended up in hell for not having pity on the poor. He did not believe it would happen. He did not bother to repent. It was a matter of faith. Life was good to him. Life is good to us. But there are many who are really struggling and perishing. We need to help them, at least one of them, if we can. For example, if each Christian family were to sponsor one child, we would make a huge impact on world poverty. I do not think that this is too much to ask for only a small amount per day.

Jesus rose from the dead. Jesus told this story. Are you convinced? The rich man said that if someone came back from the dead his brothers would be convinced. Jesus said that they only needed Moses and the prophets. We have the whole Bible! We have no excuse! We need to repent! The whole law is summarized in two statements: Love God first and foremost, and your neighbor as yourself (Matthew 22:37-40).

Is there someone you can help? Find out who. Find out how. That is your obligation. Then do it. Become someone's hero. Make an eternal difference for someone. Let the rich man's warning work for you. Heed it!

Prayer

Father, help me to see the need that is in my neighborhood, and help me know how to help meet that need. I pray in Jesus' name. Amen.

Week 48

Christians and Voting

For reading and meditation – 1 Samuel 8:6-18
"And the LORD told him: "Listen to all that the people are saying to you; it is not you they have rejected, but they have rejected me as their king." (v.7)

Will our country continue to march down the pathway of compromise with the world, rejection of Christian values and enforcement of the acceptance of ungodly practices? Or, will we stop that evil tide in its tracks and start the long road back to righteousness in the marketplace? In the United States, we have the privilege of voting to make a difference in our government.

We cannot be fatalistic about this responsibility. God is testing His people. If we fast and pray, if we act and vote and get other Christians to pray and vote, then the tide can be turned. If we fail to act, if we fail to pray, if we fail to make a difference, we will lose. We will lose our freedoms. We will lose the ability to legally oppose certain evils. We will cause our nation to

CHRISTIANS AND VOTING

begin to fall under severe judgment.

There are two great Goliath-type evils confronting our nation today that need to be turned back. One of these is the acceptance of homosexual activity. In Genesis, Lot was living amidst a similar society in Sodom. His spirit was deeply troubled by this, and yet he did not confront it. God destroyed Sodom! If our country takes a similar road, who is to say that God will not do the same to us? We can turn the tide on the acceptance of homosexual marriage with our votes and our prayers.

The other great evil is the murder of the unborn. The Bible is clear in its denunciation of violence done against the innocent. The unborn are the most innocent of all humans. Yet over a million of them have been violently murdered in our country in the last year alone, and this practice has gone on legally since 1973. We have an opportunity to stop this travesty. Even one new judge on the Supreme Court may change the balance of power enough to start the end of this inhuman practice. I think the choice is clear. If we vote for those who will enforce and back this evil, we are fellowshipping with them and participating in their sins.

We have been praying for national revival. I really want to see it. But I see two paths immediately set before us. One of them leads to the possibility of revival, where our country's very core values return to God and His ways. The other path leads to a deterioration of this country's values and ultimately to judgment. We, as voters, get to choose which path our country will follow.

I believe that a key verse for God's people in any country is 2 Chronicles 7:14, which reads, *"If my people, who are called by my name, will humble themselves and pray and seek my face and turn from their wicked ways, then will I hear from heaven and will forgive their sin and will heal their land."*

LIVING BY FAITH

    I call on you to set aside time to fast and pray. I call on you to humble yourself before God and seek Him. I call on you to confess and repent before God for whatever He brings to your heart. And I call on you to plead with God concerning our elections and their outcome. If we act, God will act. This is a critical time. What we do will make a difference. So do not just read these words, act on them.

Prayer

Father, I want to see righteousness prevail in my country. Help me to do my part. In Jesus' name I pray. Amen.

Week 49
Making Your Calling Sure

For reading and meditation – 2 Peter 1:3-11

"His divine power has given us everything we need for life and godliness…" (v.3)

One of the things I liked about President George W. Bush (U.S. President 2001-2009) was his resoluteness. He did not change his purpose about things. He set his course and stayed on it with resolve. Isaiah prophesied about Jesus the same way: *"I set my face like flint, and I know I will not be put to shame"* (Isaiah 50:7). Flint is a very hard and sharp glasslike rock that does not change its shape. Jesus achieved His purpose without ever veering from the course that was set for Him.

Our walk of faith needs to be the same. Once we know what God wants for us, we need to set our purpose and move in that direction without wavering. There are some Christians today doing just that. They are moving in the calling of God without wavering. This can only be done by faith. It can also only be done if we are sure of our calling.

Peter admonishes us to make our calling and election sure: *"Therefore, my brothers, be all the more eager to make your calling and election sure. For if you do these things, you will never fall"* (2 Peter 1:10). Our first step is to make our calling and election sure. In this verse Peter alludes to some ways to make our calling sure. He is referring to a list of qualities that we need to add to our lives, found in 2 Peter 1:5-7: *"For this very reason, make every effort to add to your faith goodness; and to goodness, knowledge; and to knowledge, self-control; and to self-control, perseverance; and to perseverance, godliness; and to godliness, brotherly kindness; and to brotherly kindness, love."*

It is these qualities of the Christian life added to your belief that will empower you to know your calling, thus allowing you to set your face like a flint to see your calling through. Now is the time to work on the qualities of the Christian faith. Once they are worked into your life, your calling will become more evident.

Peter listed seven qualities to add to faith and he mentioned them in a particular order. Are we lacking in certain areas? For example, knowledge is for me a strength. The question is, Does it outstrip my goodness? Knowledge by itself just puffs up. We need to have that foundation of goodness and faith under it for it to have value. Consequently, it is more important for new believers to add goodness to their faith, than to add knowledge. Knowledge is very important, but it has to be added in the proper order. In the end, all these characteristics need to be evident in the believer. It would be wise for us to review each of them in our own lives and resolve to work on them, in order that our calling and election become sure.

When all the qualities Peter listed are present and working in our lives, we will be people of resolve and purpose who will not be deterred from the course that God has set for us. We will

MAKING YOUR CALLING SURE

be sure of our calling, and heading in His direction for us.

A Christian teacher I know frequently asks his audiences how many of them know what their calling is in life. He gets an affirmative response from only about 10 percent of those present. This needs to change. We can change it by allowing Jesus to work on us in the areas mentioned in 2 Peter 1:5-7: faith, goodness, knowledge, self-control, perseverance, godliness, brotherly kindness, and love.

We need God's characteristics to accomplish His bidding. When we become like Him, we will set our faces like flint to do His will. His kingdom will be expanded. By faith we follow Him. When we are changed in these eight areas, our calling will be much surer than it is now. We will not be deterred from it. So let us concentrate on Him, and let Him change us. Then we will be much more effective for Him in all that we do.

Prayer

Father, show me how to pursue You in such a way that I add goodness, knowledge, self-control, perseverance, godliness, brotherly kindness, and love to my faith in order to make my calling sure. Thank you. I pray in Jesus' name. Amen.

Week 50

Fear God not Man

For reading and meditation – Exodus 20:1-20

"Moses said to the people, 'Do not be afraid. God has come to test you, so that the fear of God will be with you to keep you from sinning.'" (v.20)

Whom should we fear, God or man? Proverbs 16:6 says, *"through the fear of the LORD a man avoids evil."* Proverbs 29:25 says, *"Fear of man will prove to be a snare."* We cannot have it both ways. We either act out of fear of God, or we act out of fear of man. One way we avoid evil; the other way we are snared by it.

To fear man does not take faith. It takes faith to fear God. It takes faith to try to please God in all you do. It does not take faith to try to please man. If we fear God and live to please Him, we will find that we may also have a good reputation in the eyes of man. If, on the other hand, we only live to please man, we will be disappointed and end up compromising our values.

The Philistines put their biggest and best fighter out in front of the army to mock the Israelites. He challenged Israel to put forth a man for single combat instead of engaging the whole army. No one dared to fight him. They feared man. Even King Saul, who was head and shoulders taller than most other Israelites, refused to fight him. But David feared God rather than man. David fought Goliath and won. (Read the story in I Samuel 17.)

Another time, God gave Saul specific directions to wait at Gilgal until Samuel came and offered the sacrifice. Circumstances for Israel were dire. Saul was greatly outnumbered and his own troops were deserting. Finally, in desperation, Saul deliberately disobeyed God's command to wait, and offered the sacrifice himself. Just then Samuel appeared and rebuked him. It was the fear of man that led to Saul's downfall. Had Saul feared God more than man, he would have believed that God knew what He was doing. He would have waited as directed, even though the situation looked hopeless in the natural. (See I Samuel 10:8, 13:4-14.)

God knows what He is doing. There are many temptations in life to compromise our values because of fear. For instance, at work, your boss may ask you to compromise some value. It may be easy to rationalize, going along with him, but in the back of your mind you may be saying, "If I refuse, I will be out of a job." The fear of man has crept in. It takes courage to be true to God and His values regardless of the consequences.

True fear of God, on the other hand, brings humility. To obey is to take risk. Esther said, *"If I perish, I perish"* (Esther 4:16). We have to believe that God has our best interest in mind. We have to believe that He fully intends to take care of us, His people, and that we owe it to Him to be true to Him in every situation. The fear of God sees the judgment seat of Christ as a real place where we will account for our actions. Will our actions be based on petty fear of man and possibly our temporal well-being, or will they be based on the well-being of our soul eternally?

We get to choose and the choice is real. In 1984, I had a good position with job security. I could have stayed there until retirement. But I took a risk. I believed that God would rescue me if I believed Him, and moved in the direction I thought He was calling me. I applied to missions work overseas, and left the secure job behind.

It was one of the best choices I ever made. We never went hungry. Our children, instead of being deprived as one relative suggested, received a superb Christian education, and are all now serving the Lord.

It is worth it to fear God and follow Him. It is worth it to do what He says and demands. "*Seek first his kingdom and his righteousness, and all these things will be given to you as well*" (Matthew 6:33). If, on the other hand, we fear man, we limit God and His help. We may fall into compromise and lose our vision. Then those things we most fear may come upon us.

Only the few have ever feared God enough to be uncompromising. Be one of the few. Only the few have ever feared God enough to obey when it means sacrifice or humiliation. Be one of the few. Only the few have ever feared God enough to obey when it means risk of security. Be one of the few. Choose now to follow Jesus regardless of the cost, trusting that He will always see you through and always keep you in His loving arms.

Prayer

Father, I want to fear You more than man. I want to be one of the few uncompromisingly righteous. Give me courage. I pray in Jesus' name. Amen.

Week 51

The People God Chooses

For reading and meditation – Numbers 12:1-9

"Moses was a very humble man, more humble than anyone else on the face of the earth." (v.3)

God chose shepherds for His announcement of the Messiah's birth. God chose humble village peasants from a remote corner of the country to act as parents for His Son. God chose two very old saints, hidden from the world, to bless Jesus at the temple.

What were some things that these people God chose had in common? They had humility, they had obscurity, and they had faith. These three facts should give us a great deal of hope, as most of us have a measure of these traits.

Who does God choose today? Often, He chooses people who have humility, obscurity, and faith. Obscurity is not a character trait, but it is the condition of most people on the earth today. No one, however, is living in obscurity from God. We may think so at times, when it seems that our prayers go unanswered, but in actuality, He is present all the time. He sees us. He cares for us. He arranges our circumstances. He gives us choices. For some of the choices He presents, He even points out which choice is best. Do we always choose His way when He makes it clear to us?

We are all candidates for God to choose. In fact, He has already chosen each of us. He chose us before we were born. He has a plan for us that fits us perfectly. His plan will use our talents and interests to do what we were made to do.

Being chosen for a place in God's kingdom is great, but getting from the call to the reality is not simple. There are many obstacles along the way. The obstacles are there for a purpose, to perfect us, to build our faith. Let us take, for example, the humble peasants that God chose to be the earthly parents of Jesus. Mary faced ridicule and the shame of being unmarried and pregnant. Joseph faced the decision of what to do with Mary, his pregnant fiancée. Together they faced the journey to Bethlehem for the census during Mary's last month of pregnancy. Then there was the flight to Egypt with a small child. Being called by God did not make for an easy life. But because they had faith, they persevered.

We will also face many trials on our way to our calling. God planned it that way. The trials cause us to exercise our faith. They cause us to grow in our faith.

Sometimes waiting is the trial. Waiting may last for many years, maybe even most of your life. It was many years before Jesus grew up and started revealing Himself to the world as the Messiah. Think about Anna and Simeon. They waited their whole lives for the promise that was given to them. Their waiting paid off, as they were able to bless the infant Messiah (Luke 2:25-38).

You might say that faith in action is called patience. It is waiting for God to act. Have you ever noticed that most of the time in life, miracles are not instantaneous? Praise God for the instantaneous ones. I love to see instant healings and deliverances. However, most of what I pray for takes time, sometimes many years.

It was easy for the shepherds to be humble. It is a humble profession. If we find more prominence in life, it may become a snare to us. Do not let worldly acclaim remove your humility. People who thought highly of themselves 2000 years ago were left in the margins of the Christmas story. The same happens today. The people who think they are important are more likely to be left out of what God is doing. If anything good happens, we need to give the glory to Jesus, not take it for ourselves. Praise God that He made you and gave you your talents and gifting. Pride blinds us, and we may be taken captive by the enemy in the area where we become proud. So be on guard. Anna and Simeon remained humble all their lives, and were able to bless the Messiah in person. Let us remain humble, even when God starts using us in the way He promised.

Let us believe that God has called us. Let us stay humble, and exercise our faith. If we do, we will be amazed at what God will do in and through us.

Prayer

Father, I want to see Your plan unfold in me. Keep me humble, but let my faith grow at the same time. Help me persevere through whatever trials it takes to see Your promises realized in my life. I pray in Jesus' name. Amen.

Week 52

Servant or Friend

For reading and meditation – John 15:9-17

"You are my friends if you do what I command. I no longer call you servants, because a servant does not know his master's business. Instead, I have called you friends, for everything that I learned from my Father I have made known to you. You did not choose me, but I chose you and appointed you to go and bear fruit—fruit that will last. Then the Father will give you whatever you ask in my name." (vs.14-16)

Notice how Jesus differentiates between a servant and a friend. A servant is given chores to do by his master. The servant completes these chores without question and without knowing why he was called upon to do them. He is not given the big picture or the plan. On the other hand, a friend is not only given the tasks to accomplish, but is also given an explanation of the reasons for them. He is included in all the secrets of the operation.

Jesus calls us friends. However, only those who obey Him

are called His friends. Those who do not obey do not get to be called friends. He is the boss. If we merely obeyed, we would be servants. Some people do not obey because they refuse to stoop to be servants. With that attitude, they will never end up as friends. In Mark 10:44, Jesus said, *"whoever wants to be first must be slave of all."* Likewise, if we want to be God's friend, we must become His servant.

When we humble ourselves to service, God honors us and makes us His friends. What a beautiful thing! James 4:6 says, *"God opposes the proud but gives grace to the humble."* We think of service as drudgery. A servant, for example, is only mixing concrete all day. All he sees is the monotony of the assigned task. The friend, on the other hand, is shown the big picture. The architect takes him into the office and shows him the blueprints and the final sketches of the building. The owner of the building lets him in on his dream for its use. The friend is not just mixing concrete, he is not even just building a building, he is contributing to the life and dreams of the owner.

We are invited to be God's friends. Jesus lets us know everything the Father has revealed to Him. He does not keep anything a secret. We can know His plans and His purposes. We may be given a small role to play, but we also, along with that, are given the picture of how our small role fits into the whole plan of God.

When we are God's friends, the apparent contradictions in this passage clear up. Do we simply obey, or do we ask whatever we want? A servant only obeys. A friend, however, because he knows the master's heart, will ask for things which are also in the master's plan. We are given an understanding of the Father's plan. We are taking on the heart of Christ. We are becoming friends of God.

As friends, we become co-creators with Christ in the

carrying out and fulfillment of His plan. In so doing, we are asking for what we already believe is the Father's will. If a worker understood not only about how to mix concrete, but also about the uses and function of the final product, he might actually have ideas to make the building better, improving on the original design. In like manner, we can actually have input with the Father about the shape of the kingdom that He is building.

Two required elements are very important in the life of believers. The first is a living relationship with the Father. In this relationship, we hear from Him everyday. We read the Bible on a regular basis and believe that God speaks to us through it. The second element is faith. We need to believe that what we do really does make a difference for the kingdom of God. We need to believe that God really did assign the winning of the world to people filled with the Holy Spirit.

When we have these two elements working in us, and we are obedient to what we think God is asking us to do, then we will truly be God's friends. We will be able to ask for anything in Jesus' name and receive it. We will bear much fruit for the kingdom.

Prayer

Father, I want to be Your friend. Help me to be obedient in all things, and seek to know Your heart. I pray in Jesus' name. Amen.

Week 53

Faith and Weakness

For reading and meditation – Matthew 26:36-46

"Watch and pray so that you will not fall into temptation. The spirit is willing, but the body is weak." (v.41)

Too many times we complain, "I cannot do anything for Christ; I am weak. That job needs someone who is strong!" The Bible teaches the contrary. Jesus took on human weakness. He walked as a weak human. He died as a weak human. Yet through it all, He lived a sinless life, perfectly fulfilling the Father's calling for Him on earth. 2 Corinthians 13:4 says, *"For to be sure, he was crucified in weakness, yet he lives by God's power. Likewise, we are weak in him, yet by God's power we will live with him to serve you."*

We are all weak. We know we are weak. Who is the man or woman that God chooses? Is it the strong? 1 Corinthians 1:26-28 says, *"Brothers, think of what you were when you were called. Not many of you were wise by human standards; not many were influential; not many were of noble birth. But God chose the foolish things of the world to shame the wise; God chose the weak things of the world to shame the strong. He chose the lowly things of this world and the despised things—and the things that are not—to nullify the things that are."* God does not choose people based on their natural abilities. Paul boasted about His weakness: *"But he said to me, 'My grace is sufficient for you, for my power is made perfect in weakness.' Therefore I will boast all the more gladly about my weaknesses, so that Christ's power may rest on me. That is why, for Christ's sake, I delight in weaknesses, in insults, in hardships, in persecutions, in difficulties. For when I am weak, then I am strong"* (2 Corinthians 12:9-10). Being weak makes us good candidates to be used for God's purposes for the advancement of His kingdom. We all qualify!

The reason God chooses the weak is so that His power will come through and be recognized. It is so we who are chosen will be forced to rely on Him. We give Him the glory. If we are weak, it is obvious to us that He has to do the true spiritual work or it will not get done. We are prime candidates for God to choose.

Let us look at one of the people God chose, a fisherman named Simon. He usually blurted out whatever was on his mind. He acted without thinking. He had fears. He almost started a war that would have gotten the whole band of disciples killed. At the crucial moment when He should have shown strength, He denied that He ever knew Christ. On his own, Peter was weak. But God filled Him with the Holy Spirit and empowered Him. In the end, Peter was strong, but it was God's power, not his.

We still need to develop our talents. We need to hone our abilities. All giftings are from God. But no matter how well-honed our natural abilities are, they are powerless when it comes to doing anything for God. We need to acknowledge

FAITH AND WEAKNESS

that no matter what our talents are, there is another necessary element. We need to take upon ourselves His strength. With His strength we can do all things. With His strength, our talents can make a difference.

All that we do can be energized by God. Isaiah 40:31 says, *"but those who hope in the LORD will renew their strength. They will soar on wings like eagles; they will run and not grow weary, they will walk and not be faint."* We begin walking in His strength rather than our own weakness when we put our hope in Jesus, when we seek Him with all our heart, when we listen to what He has to say to us and obey it, and when we give Him the credit for what is done. In His strength we will see the hand of God working through us in mighty ways.

Regardless of your present set of talents or lack thereof, you are a candidate for ministry. Acknowledge your lack of strength. Seek God and His strength. He can and will empower anyone who comes to Him with a sincere heart for a part in the building of His kingdom. That is good news! You can have a powerful, positive impact on the people in your world.

Prayer

Father, I acknowledge that I am weak. I want to exchange my weakness for Your strength. I give You all the glory. I pray in Jesus' name. Amen.

Week 54

Faith and Zeal

For reading and meditation – John 2:12-25

"So he made a whip out of cords, and drove all from the temple area, both sheep and cattle; he scattered the coins of the money changers and overturned their tables. To those who sold doves he said, 'Get these out of here! How dare you turn my Father's house into a market!' His disciples remembered that it is written: 'Zeal for your house will consume me.'" (vs.15-17)

Nearly every time zeal is mentioned in the Bible, it refers to someone who takes violent action against his enemies. Properly directed zeal is required for God's kingdom to come in greater measure here on earth. Sometimes zeal is misdirected. Proverbs 19:2 says, *"It is not good to have zeal without knowledge, nor to be hasty and miss the way."* The apostle Paul, before his conversion, had a great deal of zeal for God in persecuting the church. His zeal was misdirected.

Zeal is like a burning fire. It is a passion that consumes. Jeremiah described it as fire in his bones (Jeremiah 20:9). It is

FAITH AND ZEAL

a fire that requires not only action but intense action, focused action. It requires something to change.

What does it take for us to become zealous? How long will we drift along in lukewarmness like the Laodicean church in Revelation 3:16? Zeal is always hot. Any time any significant advance to the kingdom of God has taken place, there were zealous people involved. Zealous people dare to risk everything for the cause of Christ. Zealous people put everything else on hold except for the cause of Christ.

When I read about John the Baptist, I see a man with a singular focus! He was zealous for the coming of the kingdom. I saw a movie about Martin Luther. One characteristic that made a difference for him was his passion, his zeal. He would not back down from the truth for any man. Every revival in history has been preceded by people of zeal and passion who have cried out to God relentlessly for Him to act until He did. They would not take "no" for an answer.

If we want to see a revival in our area, we must become passionate people. We must become zealously and totally committed. At the same time, we must make sure that our zeal is properly directed.

Here are some pointers toward experiencing properly directed zeal.

One: **Feeding**. We need to learn the scriptures. We also need to hear from God daily. This means regular times in the Bible. When you read the Bible, make sure that you ask God to speak to you. It is not just a contest to see how much you can read, it is a spiritual meal. Also read other Christian literature. I read Christian literature every day, whether it be a book or a magazine article, or something on the internet. This will also feed you. It will keep you from becoming zealous without knowledge, which is dangerous.

Two: **Fellowship**. You can keep a fire hot by keeping it together. If you move a stick out of the fire it cools off. In the same way, if you stay away from true heart-to-heart fellowship with other believers, you will tend to cool off. To stay hot for Jesus, go to where others are passionate for Him and stay connected there. Zeal is contagious.

Three: **Focus**. Keep your eyes on Jesus. Spend much time worshipping Him. Let Him direct your actions. See the end of your faith, the salvation of your soul. When He speaks, obey. Those with zeal all had a focus on one goal. The apostle Paul said it best: *"I press on toward the goal to win the prize for which God has called me heavenward in Christ Jesus"* (Philippians 3:14).

If you attend to these three things: *feeding, fellowship,* and *focus,* then you will begin to *fire* up in zeal. Your life will begin to *flower* for the Lord. You will start *flowing* in *fruitful* ministry. You will become a *flaming* arrow for the Lord, *flying* accurately for His target for your life, and you will *forge* a *flourishing, forceful flow* of God's Spirit!

Prayer

Father, I want my zeal for You increased. Help me to get more feeding, fellowship, and focus to move me towards the passion that I need in my life to make a difference for You. I pray in Jesus' name. Amen.

Week 55

Faith and Unity

For reading and meditation – Ephesians 4:11-16

"It was he who gave some to be apostles, some to be prophets, some to be evangelists, and some to be pastors and teachers, to prepare God's people for works of service, so that the body of Christ may be built up until we all reach unity in the faith and in the knowledge of the Son of God and become mature, attaining to the whole measure of the fullness of Christ." (vs.11-13)

How do we achieve unity in the faith? This is one of the primary things that God wants to see in the church. God will unify His church. In order for that to happen, we have to grow up in Christ. That growing is both individually and corporately across the entire body of Christ. This is an impossible task for any person or ministry. It is only God in His sovereignty who will carry it out, but He needs our cooperation.

Unity does not mean that we believe every little thing the same. That is uniformity. God is a God of diversity. Philippians 2:12 says to *"work out your salvation with fear and trembling."*

There are at least four levels of doctrine. Critical doctrines are those that all true believers hold, such as the resurrection of Jesus, the virgin birth, His sinless life, and His atonement for our sins. These doctrines separate Christians from non-Christians. The next level down separates denominations. These beliefs have to do with such things as modes of baptism and how the Holy Spirit works. They are important enough for us to choose one church over another, but we still acknowledge those in the other churches to be believers. On the next level down, we can actually attend the same church and differ in beliefs such as what happens in the end times and which version of the Bible to use. The fourth level is the personal level, where we choose things for ourselves that we do not think need to be imposed on others.

We can have unity of the Spirit without ever coming to unity of doctrine. We will never come to complete unity of doctrine in this life. Our doctrines, however, will start coming closer together as we draw closer to Jesus. Unity is in Jesus. As we focus on Him and our life in Him, we have fellowship with one another in unity.

If, on the other hand, we focus on differences, we will never come to unity. A photon, which is the smallest packet of light that can exist, has a dual nature. If a photon is measured as a particle, it is a particle. If it is measured as a wave, it is a wave. It cannot be measured as both at once. If you are looking for a wave, you get that and nothing else. If you are looking for a particle, you get that and nothing else. That is the dual nature of light as documented in physics. Yet we all live with this paradox every day, and could not live without it. There are many such spiritual paradoxes. Often, these are the things which divide us doctrinally. As we grow closer to Jesus, we will see Him in a more multifaceted way.

FAITH AND UNITY

Unity can be reached in at least three ways. **First**, focus on Jesus. He is the author and finisher of our faith. Always see everyone and everything through the eyes of Christ. Stay tuned to the Spirit. As much as depends on you, live in peace and harmony with everyone (Romans 12:18). The first way is to focus on Jesus and live in tune with the Holy Spirit.

The **second** way to achieve unity is to do works of service. Those who serve Him become more unified with others who serve Him. This is a mystery! It is in doing these works that we come into unity. God has given each one a ministry to someone somewhere. It is in carrying out that ministry that you come into unity with other believers.

The **third** way to achieve unity is to be built up in knowledge of the Son of God. We need to press in to know the Lord Jesus personally in a love relationship. Then our unity with other Christians will be built.

Spend time with God every day. Read your Bible. Pray. Have fellowship often. Find some ministry this week that you can do for someone. Receive teaching from a ministry regularly. Do all this, and you will find your unity with other believers increasing.

Prayer

Father, help me to focus more on You, do works of service, and receive ministry so that I will be unified more with You and Your people. I pray in Jesus' name. Amen.

Week 56

Faith and God's Timing

For reading and meditation – 2 Peter 1:1-11

"His divine power has given us everything we need for life and godliness..." (v.3)

We know that God's timing is perfect. However, it is often not the timing that we would like! We want instantaneous results; God wants eternal results. We want to see how we can do something before we start. God wants us to trust Him with the impossible.

God told Abram that He would give the land of Canaan to his descendants (Genesis 12:6). Abram believed God. The years passed and nothing happened. Abram and Sarai were too old to have children. Abram's faith was tried and he took matters into his own hands. Abram, at age 85, had a child with Hagar, his wife's servant, after waiting ten years. It was another fourteen years before God came through with the son of promise and the name change to Abraham.

When God speaks, we will be tempted to finish in the flesh

FAITH AND GOD'S TIMING

what He started in the Spirit. The apostle Paul warns us not to do it that way (Galatians 3:3). What we start in the Spirit, we need to finish in the Spirit. If we get side-tracked, we need to repent, and return to relying on God. God did not reject Abram because he produced a son of the flesh. He had mercy on him and fulfilled His word in spite of Abram's wrong choice. In like manner, He will have mercy on us and fulfill His word in us, even if we have disobeyed.

Our faith in God will grow as we wait in faith for His timing. Even if the wait is long, there comes a time when God's time is *now*. His will always happens at a *now* time. We only live in the present. We need to trust Him *now* for the future.

For many years, I knew that God was going to send me overseas at some time in the future. When the U.S. Air Force sent me to Thailand in 1975, I visited some local missionaries. It was then I realized that their kind of lifestyle and work would not fit me very well, so I put the dream out of my mind. It seemed to die, just like Abraham's dream. Later, when I was a young school teacher, I spent years trying to figure out a way to change my profession, because I was having a hard time with it. Finally, after five years of teaching, I came to peace with my profession. I said to myself that I could continue teaching until retirement. As soon as I was able to say that, God spoke to me. He said it was time to go overseas.

Sometimes God's time is when the preliminary work is done in us. He waited until I was ready. There were things in me that needed doing first. As soon as they were accomplished, He could send me. Sometimes it works that way.

When God said it was time to go, we had no time to lose. Within a year, we were in the Philippines. We stayed there for fifteen years, until our job there was finished. When we returned to the U.S.A., God said that there would be a promotion. I thought it would be right away, but God does not work that way. There has been a delay. He did not tell me that there would be a training period before the promotion. These intervening years have been in preparation for whatever the promotion is going to be. When the time comes, it may again be sudden. However, He must first prepare me fully for it.

Sometimes God's timing seems delayed. Do you think that God really wanted the children of Israel to wander for forty years in the wilderness? The twelve spies went up to spy out the land. If they had come back with faith, they could have gone in immediately (Numbers 13-14). But it took forty years in the desert to refine them and make them ready to take their inheritance. They left Egypt fleeing for their lives from their enemy. When their children were finally ready to go into the promised land, their enemies melted with fear before them.

There have been Joshuas and Calebs telling us all these years that we can take the land if we only believe. I believe that the time is rapidly approaching when we will take them up on it, believe God's promises, and take our city, our state, our nation, and our world for the gospel. The time of rapid deployment is approaching. Do you want to be a part? The time of waiting is nearly over. Get ready!

Prayer

Father, thank You that You are preparing us for a mission. Help me to quickly become ready for Your next step in my life. I pray in Jesus' name. Amen!

Week 57
Listening for God's Voice

For reading and meditation – John 10:1-30

"My sheep listen to my voice; I know them, and they follow me."
(v.27)

Everyone hears God's voice. He speaks in nature. He speaks in our hearts. He speaks through our circumstances. He speaks through scripture. He speaks through others. He may speak loudly or in whispers. There may be many other ways that He speaks.

The real question is not, "Do you hear God's voice?" It is, "Do you *listen* to it, believe it, and obey it? What is He saying to *you*?"

To us Christians, God speaks the most loudly when we are off course, when we have sinned. When we give in to temptation, even just a little, God starts speaking to us. Giving in to temptation just a little may lead to worse offenses. If we continue to stray, the Holy Spirit will shout at us: "Look out! Danger! Don't go there!" If we still do not listen, we will allow the enemy of our souls to hurt us. Then, as we harden our hearts, our hearing may stop working as well. It will become harder for us to return to the path of life.

God delights to lead us to repentance. But it takes humility for us to admit we deliberately sinned, and need to repent and ask for forgiveness. We had better listen when God talks loudly to us. If we wait too long, we may not hear.

If God wanted to, He could keep us from sinning altogether. If He did that, He would be overruling our hearts. Then, He would not have our hearts. God wants our hearts. That is why He lets us choose our own ways. He then calls us back to Himself when we stray. We have to return to Him in our hearts. If we truly love God more than our sin, we will return to Him and turn away from the sin.

God wants to speak to us all the time, not just when we sin. He has a plan for the whole world. He wants to talk to each one of us about His plan for the whole world. He wants to give us orders about our role in winning the world for Christ, about advancing the kingdom of God. He can only do this if He does not have to continually concentrate on the healings that are needed in our own lives. We need to care for our relationship with Him so that we can concentrate on our assigned task in the kingdom.

There are stages in how God speaks to us, His sheep.

First, He speaks about our sin. This is the loudest and most important speech. Listen. This speech will bring us into right relationship with God.

Second, He speaks to us about our sanctification, or what we must do and learn to become more like Him. This speech will make us useful to God for the advancement of His kingdom. Many people of God never get through this phase. It is the phase where God moves in our lives so that our lives line up with our beliefs. Much fruit can come through us as we become like Jesus and obey Him.

Third, He speaks to us about His plans for us for the advancement of His kingdom. Our focus is no longer on our own sanctification, but on the mission of the church. This phase happens simultaneously with the previous one.

We are most effective for the gospel when we hear His orders for us to do something for someone else. He calls on us to pray for others. He calls on us to care for the poor. He calls on us to make disciples. When we are no longer absorbed with our own concerns, we are most useful for the kingdom.

God is speaking. What is He saying to me? What is He saying to you? Is He asking you to clean up your life? Is He dealing with issues in your life? Or is He giving you plans for the advancement of the kingdom? Maybe He is doing all three. God is speaking to you today. Listen to, believe in, and obey Him!

Prayer

Father, I want to be effective for You. Help me to conquer my personal issues quickly so that I can be a more useful servant. I pray in Jesus' name. Amen.

―― Week 58 ――

Faith and Opposition

For reading and meditation – Genesis 26: 1-33

"Isaac planted crops in that land and the same year reaped a hundredfold, because the LORD blessed him. The man became rich, and his wealth continued to grow until he became very wealthy. He had so many flocks and herds and servants that the Philistines envied him. So all the wells that his father's servants had dug in the time of his father Abraham, the Philistines stopped up, filling them with earth. Then Abimelech said to Isaac, 'Move away from us; you have become too powerful for us.' So Isaac moved away from there and encamped in the Valley of Gerer and settled there." (vs.12-17)

Abraham was a man of war. Isaac, his son, was a man of peace. Abraham boldly acted in obedience to God. Isaac humbly submitted to the will of God. Isaac was blessed by God even when he did not resist the opposition that was constantly standing in his path. God had promised that all the nations of the earth would be blessed through Isaac. In like manner, God wants to

FAITH AND OPPOSITION

bless us and our world through us. God wants to bless us so we can bless others.

With blessing comes a problem. The Philistines became jealous. In their envy, they filled up the wells Isaac inherited from his father. Water was a very critical commodity for Isaac, since he was a sheep herder. I know that in the west of this country, the ranchers would practically go to war against each other for water. Stopping up wells was very serious. If you were Isaac and someone stopped up your wells, what would you do?

Isaac, the man of peace, did not go to war with the Philistines. He may have had every right to, but he did not. Jesus said, *"If someone strikes you on the right cheek, turn to him the other also"* (Matthew 5:39). Isaac did not go to war, he went to work. He dug another well and just kept going. He believed that it was God who had blessed him. It was not his own work, so when he was knocked down, he did not strike out at or lay blame on anyone, he just went to work and reopened the well. By God's grace, we can do the same.

When God blesses us there will be opposition. There will be those who deliberately put hindrances in our way. We may have every right to take action against them, but that is not the Christian way. Jesus said to turn the other cheek. The proper action is to keep digging.

That was not the end of Isaac's trouble. He decided to dig his own well, not just unstop those dug by his father. As soon as he finished one, there was a dispute with the local herdsmen for the water. He gave in and gave them the well. Then he dug another. The dispute was repeated and again, Isaac gave in. Finally, on the third attempt, he was left alone.

I am amazed at Isaac's perseverance in the face of opposition. He could have fought or given up at any point. But how are you going to win your enemies to Christ if you fight them?

At the same time we say, "But we cannot let them walk all over us!" Apparently, Isaac did. Relationship and accommodating others and keeping the peace were more important to him than demanding his rights. He believed by faith that God would take care of the problem.

In America we seem to spend too much energy demanding our rights. Demanding our rights comes at the price of relationships with others and peace with others. Which of these is really more important? I think the Bible is showing in this passage that relationships and peace with others are more important than our rights.

God is the one who blessed Isaac. He lost no relationships, but rather made friends by giving away a couple wells, and he lived in peace among all. We can trust God for the same. The next time someone blocks what is rightfully yours, remember Isaac, who just went to work and dug another well. In the end, he was blessed and he made friends of his enemies all around.

Prayer

Father, I pray that You will give me the faith of Isaac, not demanding my own rights, but rather trusting You for Your blessing. I pray in Jesus' name. Amen.

Week 59

Faith and Words

For reading and meditation – Matthew 12:22-37

"I tell you that men will have to give account on the day of judgment for every careless word they have spoken. For by your words you will be acquitted, and by your words you will be condemned." (vs.36-37)

We can be fooled by words of others some of the time, but God is never fooled. He knows just what we mean. He knows exactly what it is in our heart that motivates the words. Jesus was never fooled. No one could catch Him in His words, because He was pure inside. He caught many because He knew what was in their hearts.

It is possible to appear clean on the outside while the inside is still filthy. Modern professionals are taught techniques in smooth persuasive communication. These methods make it appear that the heart of the speaker is good, whether it is or not. There are ways to make it look like you care, thus winning the trust of the listener, when you are actually manipulating the client for your benefit.

Even when these communication styles are used, the professional is speaking from the abundance of his heart. The client may be fooled, however, about the speaker's true motivation. I have fallen for this trap several times and it always, in the end, leaves a bad taste in my mouth. That is because the true designs finally come out. By then the damage is done.

We will have to give account for our words. Our careful words are the ones that fool people some of the time. But we will also have to give account for our careless words. The careless words are the ones that just come out. They just surface in conversation or when we are called on to talk impromptu, or when we hear bad news, or when bad things happen to us.

Take some time and listen to your careless words. What are you saying? What are you saying about yourself, about God, about faith, about others, about our final destination? I listen to public school students' careless talk when I am at work. Most of it is harmful rather than helpful.

We could even take this little experiment back one further step. We can listen to the unvoiced comments that flow through our mind. Whether we say them or just have a script running through our head, these words are important for us to consider.

If I am going to give account of my words on the judgment day, I might want to do some evaluating now to see how I am doing. It will not take long before I realize that my script is not holy all the time.

Too much of the time, I find my mind wandering off onto dirty topics that I would never want to voice. This can happen right in the middle of a sermon or a prayer. *"What a wretched man I am! Who will rescue me from this body of death?"* (Romans 7:24)

FAITH AND WORDS

The way to clean up our thoughts and our speech is to saturate ourselves with the things of God. We need to set our minds *"on things above, not on earthly things"* (Colossians 3:2). In so doing, we need to *"put to death, therefore, whatever belongs to [our] earthly nature"* (Colossians 3:5).

Every day we need to focus on the Bible, hear from God, pray, praise, pray in the spirit, have some fellowship, and read the scripture. If we limit these activities to one day per week, our thoughts and speech will not stay as clean. Jesus cleans up our heart as we focus on Him and seek Him.

Being cleaned on the inside is not an easy or short process, but we should see progress over time. My thoughts are no longer continually as vile as they were in my "before Christ" days, but they are not yet continually pure. He is working on me. One of the ways I evaluate that working is by listening to my internal scripts and my careless words. You can do the same.

It is the inside we want cleaned up, not just the words. The world is satisfied with just cleaning up the words, but that is not good enough. Jesus' main complaint with the Pharisees was that they only cleaned up the outside of the cup, leaving the inside filthy. (See Matthew 23:25) We must not do this. We must allow Jesus to clean us from the inside out.

Prayer

Father, I pray that You would reveal to me how my life needs cleaning up, and then empower me to do so. I pray in Jesus' name. Amen.

Week 60

Faith and the Blood

For reading and meditation – Hebrews 9:11-28
"Without the shedding of blood there is no forgiveness." (v.22)

How do we receive forgiveness for our sins? We are only saved because Jesus shed His blood and gave His life for us. Although it may be difficult to understand why it took the shedding of the blood of the Son of God to free us from sin, this concept is a theme that is found all the way through the Bible.

In the Garden of Eden, when Adam and Eve sinned, they covered themselves with fig leaves, but the Lord clothed them in animal skins. The blood of the animals was a type and shadow of the shedding of Christ's blood. Fig leaves, representing Adam and Eve's own works, were not enough.

In the next generation, Abel brought animal sacrifices to God while Cain brought only crops (see Genesis 4). When Abraham went to sacrifice Isaac, God stopped him at the last minute. God then provided a ram to sacrifice (Genesis 22:13). At the Passover, the lamb was sacrificed and its blood smeared

FAITH AND THE BLOOD

on the doorpost, so that the death angel would pass over and not strike dead the firstborn who lived in that house (Exodus 12:12-13).

The tabernacle and the temple were designed as places for animal sacrifices to be carried out on a regular basis. There were prescriptions in the law for the sacrifice of certain animals for various reasons. Consequently, there was a thriving business of the selling of sheep and doves and other animals in the court of the temple.

Pagan religions had sacrifices of animals and even human sacrifices to their gods. Where did they get this practice? It is a copy of the pattern set up by God. The devil is a great imitator.

Shortly after Jesus died for us, the temple in Jerusalem was destroyed and all the animal sacrifices stopped. They are no longer necessary. The sacrifice of animals was never good enough to cleanse sin. Otherwise, it would not have been repeated over and over. Only the blood of Jesus is enough. It is so good, that He only had to die once for us all, for all time.

All people saved from the beginning of time to the end of time are saved the same way, by the blood of Jesus. Adam was saved by the blood of Jesus. Moses was saved by the blood of Jesus. Abraham was saved by the blood of Jesus. David was saved by the blood of Jesus. All the Old Testament saints were saved by grace, not works. They all believed in God's coming provision, and the Lord counted it as righteousness. Although they did not have nearly the understanding that we do of the Messiah, they are only accountable for the degree of revelation that they had. They lived in a world of types and shadows. The rituals they practiced were only shadows of the heavenly reality.

We, who have more light, need to live in that greater light.

LIVING BY FAITH

They did not have the New Testament; we do. They did not know the story of Jesus; we do. Only a very few of them were filled with the Holy Spirit, since it was not given until Pentecost. The world is filled with far more light now than it was then. We need to live in that light.

We commemorate the shedding of Jesus' blood whenever we take communion. He said, *"this is My body, which is broken for you"* (1 Corinthians 11:24 KJV) when giving us the bread, and, *"This cup is the new testament in My blood"* (1 Corinthians 11:25 KJV) when giving us the cup. His blood has already been shed. It was sufficient. Our sins are gone. We only need to celebrate, and to remember what He did for us.

We do not need to understand it. I am a logical thinker. I cannot understand the shedding of blood for the forgiveness of sins by using logic. I can only believe it by faith. Because it cannot be deduced logically, it can be a stumbling block. It is a stumbling block to the lost, but to us who are going from victory to victory, the shedding of Jesus' blood for us is light and life. We must believe it by faith. God decreed it from the beginning. He foreshadowed it, He carried it out, and now we commemorate it. We are not called to understand how it works, but just to believe that it does. The blood of Jesus is sufficient for salvation for all who believe, from Adam to the end of the world. Hallelujah!

Prayer

Father, thank You that my sins are gone. Thank You for the blood of Jesus that cleansed me. Thank You in Jesus' name. Amen.

Week 61

Faith and Your Comfort Zone

For reading and meditation – Matthew 10:16-26

"I am sending you out like sheep among wolves." (v.16)

The American way is to work hard so that we can sit back and be comfortable. Unfortunately, the comfortable Christian is probably not very effective for God. The Christians were comfortable at Laodicea, but God said, *"I know your deeds, that you are neither cold nor hot. I wish you were either one or the other!"* (Revelation 3:15). If we want to be effective for God, we need to fan the flame of faith in our hearts. Then our deeds will be done with more zeal. When God sees that we have zeal for Him, He will ask us to do something that will stretch our faith. It may move us into a place of discomfort. Fan the flame and get ready for God to ask you to enlarge your comfort zone!

God wants to expand us, to cause us to grow. He also wants us to become a part of His work on the earth. There are many examples in the Bible where ordinary people were called to step out in faith into a very uncomfortable position. Because they did so, God was glorified and the kingdom was advanced.

God called Moses at the burning bush (see Exodus 3). He told him to go back to Egypt and speak to Pharaoh, asking him to let the Hebrews leave Egypt. The idea of leading millions of people and the idea of speaking to Pharaoh were both very uncomfortable to Moses. What if Moses had refused? But Moses did not refuse. He did what God called him to do. Because Moses stepped out of his comfort zone, Israel was delivered.

Esther needed to take an urgent message to her husband the king. To enter his presence unbidden was dangerous. If the king did not hold out the scepter, then the penalty for entering his presence without being summoned was death. Esther entered the king's presence unbidden anyway, disregarding her own life. It was definitely out of her comfort zone (see Esther 4 and 5). Because she did this, Israel was saved.

Ananias was called by God to meet Saul at Straight Street in Antioch. Ananias had heard about Saul. Saul was a murderer of Christians. Ananias stepped far out of his comfort zone and obeyed. Saul was able to enter his ministry as a result (see Acts 9:10-22).

Peter had a vision on the roof in which he saw unclean animals and God told him to kill and eat them. The vision was not about eating animals; it was actually about gentiles coming to Jesus and being accepted in the kingdom. Peter stepped out of his comfort zone and preached the gospel to the gentiles (See Acts 10).

All through history, the saints of God have been called away from their life of leisure to the uncomfortable, in order to advance the kingdom.

St. Francis of Assisi was the son of a wealthy cloth dyer. He could have lived a life of ease, yet he chose to step out of his comfort zone and live entirely for God, giving up the life

FAITH AND YOUR COMFORT ZONE

of ease.

Sometimes we are faced with that very choice. Do we maintain our comfortable status quo, not rocking the boat? Or do we take a risk, stepping out of the boat to go and do whatever Jesus wants? Do we pray Isaiah's prayer, *"Here am I. Send me!"* (Isaiah 6:8)? Or, do we make excuses about why we cannot or will not go?

There is no sin so bad that Jesus' death did not deal with it. There is no condition so bad that He cannot speak to it or minister to it. However, Jesus expects us, His followers, to be His hands and feet on the earth. He speaks through us. He ministers through us. We need to be willing to speak and minister wherever He chooses. When we are, we will find that He chooses for us to speak and minister in places and situations that are out of our comfort zone, stretching and changing us.

Isn't that the way we want it to happen? He prepares and sends us. He tells us what to do and then He does it through us, so He gets all the glory. We think that what He is asking us to do is too difficult or uncomfortable, and yet He helps us all the way.

Do not resist or hold back. When God calls you to do something for Him that you know you cannot do, jump in with both feet and trust Him to be with you all the way. Watch the miracles unfold!

Prayer

Father, give me courage to step out in boldness when You call me to work for You in ways that are uncomfortable for me. I pray in Jesus' name. Amen!

Week 62

Giving by Faith

For reading and meditation – Genesis 4:1-16

"Now Abel kept flocks, and Cain worked the soil. In the course of time Cain brought some of the fruits of the soil as an offering to the LORD. But Abel brought fat portions from some of the firstborn of his flock. The LORD looked with favor on Abel and his offering, but on Cain and his offering he did not look with favor."
(vs.2-5)

When we give, we do it by faith, trusting God to see us through to the next paycheck. We should not wait to the end of the next pay period to see if there is anything left to give.

The above verses reveal why God looked with favor on the offering of Abel and not on the offering of Cain. Abel gave with faith and Cain did not. Abel brought generous portions of the first fruits of his flock. Abel took the first and best and brought it to the Lord. Abel did not wait to the end of the month to see if he had enough to pay his bills; he gave before he was sure of having enough. He gave to God first, and trusted Him for

GIVING BY FAITH

the rest.

On the other hand, the verse above says that *"in the course of time Cain brought some of the fruits..."* Cain did not bring the first fruits. Cain waited. My guess is that he waited until he was sure he had enough to provide until the next season. Then he looked and saw that there was some extra, and gave some of that to God. Giving does not take any faith when it is done that way. God did not accept Cain's offering because it was not mixed with faith. Instead of putting God first, Cain gave God the leftovers. Cain believed in God and wanted to please Him, but Cain did not trust Him. His lack of trust was evident in the way that he gave.

I have been guilty of the same sin on occasion. There have been times when I have carefully counted to see how much money would be left at the end of the pay period so I would know how much I could afford to give to God. That is not faith. No matter how much I give, if I give in that manner, I am not exercising faith in God's provision. God calls us to give the first fruits of all we receive, which means that when the check comes in, we take off the tithe first, before even looking at the stack of bills. God honors that kind of faith.

The whole Bible is full of this kind of giving. The most important one is found in Romans 5:8 where it reads, *But God demonstrates his own love for us in this: While we were still sinners, Christ died for us."* God the father sacrificed his son, Jesus, for us before anyone was saved. He was sacrificed first. It was done in faith that many would believe and be saved.

This kind of love is not quite the same as taking the first ten percent and giving it. It is much more radical. God gave His all. It was His only plan to redeem mankind. He did it up front and first, before anyone was saved. God demonstrated the way to faith.

LIVING BY FAITH

In like manner, we show God that we trust Him by giving of the first fruits of our substance, rather than waiting until we see if there is anything left to give. What if God had waited to see if any were good enough to deserve dying for? No one would be saved.

We need not only to give our tithes and offerings, but we need to do it as first fruits. We should not wait to see if there is enough left over for us, but exercise our faith and give first. Then God will accept our offering and multiply it for His use, and we will be blessed in the process.

Prayer

Father, help me to trust You by giving to You off the top of my paycheck and not waiting to see if I have enough. I ask in Jesus' name. Amen.

Week 63

Multiplication

For reading and meditation – Galatians 6:7-10

"A man reaps what he sows." (v.7)

Tithing is not the same as giving. If I let you borrow my car and you drove it for a while, I would expect you to eventually return it to me. What if you came back to me and said, "I'm giving you this car. Here are the keys." How preposterous! It was not yours to give. You were just returning to me what was already mine. You should have said, "Thank you, and by the way, I put gas in it and washed it for you."

We do just such a preposterous thing to God. Leviticus 27:30 says, *"A tithe of everything from the land, whether grain from the soil or fruit from the trees, belongs to the LORD; it is holy to the LORD."* God already owns the tenth or tithe. Therefore, when we bring that amount, we are not giving, but returning back to God what already belongs to Him. We are to do this with thankfulness. When we do this much, He will bless the other 90 percent so that it will be enough. It will stretch to cover all that we need.

Giving offerings actually starts after the tithe is already returned to God. If you thought you were giving offerings of the first tenth, you were mistaken. When you give your tithes, God will make sure you have enough.

When you go beyond the tithe, there will be abundance. The principle of multiplication will begin to work in your finances. This principle works only for those who give offerings to God. Remember, the first tenth does not count; God already owns that. It comes into effect when you give what God does not claim. When you start giving some of that remaining 90 percent, God will notice and multiply it.

Jesus noticed when the widow gave all she had, only two mites (see Mark 12:42). Jesus defended Mary when she gave expensive perfume worth a year's wages, and just poured it out on His feet (see John 12:3-8).

The principle of sowing and reaping applies when you give. You sow your gift into the kingdom. Where there is sowing, there will always be reaping. There is a harvest coming from your sowing, your giving over and above the tithe. Those who sow are also partakers of the harvest. That is how the principle of multiplication works.

When you sow over and above your tithe, then some of that harvest comes back to you, so you can sow some more. In the parable of the talents (Matthew 25:14-29), one man received five talents, another received two talents, and the third, just one talent. The man who received five returned his five to the master along with five more. The first five he returned already belonged to his master. It was like the tithe. But he gave back more. It was the same with the man who received two talents. In each case there was a reward for giving over and above what was required. But the man who only returned what was

MULTIPLICATION

rightfully the master's was rebuked. It is almost as if there is a rebuke for those who only tithe, who only return to God what is rightfully His in the first place.

The question is simple: Do you want to see abundant blessing and multiplication in your life? Then start giving over and above the amount that rightfully belongs to God. But do not give for that reason. Give because you want to see the kingdom of God enlarging and expanding in the world. God will notice your giving. He will say, "Look! There is a giver. I will bless him so that he can give more."

There are many examples of people who give very high percentages of their income. They did not start out that way, but they did start out by giving over and above the tithe. Then, as God blessed them, they were able to give a higher and higher percentage. There are some people, who near the end of their lives, are regularly giving ninety percent and keeping only ten percent to live on.

You will never find out if what I have said is true or not unless you act on it. That takes faith. Is the Bible true? If your answer is "yes," then act on it and give. You will be glad you did!

PRAYER

Father, give me the courage to give over and above the tithe.
Help me to do it joyfully. I pray in Jesus' name. Amen.

Week 64

Faith and Pentecost

For reading and meditation – Acts 2

"When the day of Pentecost came, they were all together in one place. Suddenly a sound like the blowing of a violent wind came from heaven and filled the whole house where they were sitting."
(vs.1-2)

The feast of Pentecost celebrates several different events in the Old Testament. Traditionally, the law was given to Moses on Mt. Sinai on the day of Pentecost. Another name for Pentecost was the Feast of Harvest. This feast came at the end of the wheat harvest. At the end of the harvest, the people would give an offering to the Lord. This festival was also called the Feast of Weeks, because it was seven weeks from Passover to Pentecost.

After His resurrection, Jesus spoke to his disciples saying: *"Do not leave Jerusalem, but wait for the gift my Father promised, which you have heard me speak about. For John baptized with water, but in a few days you will be baptized with the Holy Spirit.... you will receive power when the Holy Spirit comes on*

FAITH AND PENTECOST

you; and you will be my witnesses in Jerusalem, and in all Judea and Samaria, and to the ends of the earth" (Acts 1:4-8). Jesus was raised at Passover. Seven weeks later, the church was born during the wheat harvest at Pentecost. This time God sent the Holy Spirit, putting the law in the hearts of the people, rather than on stone tablets as He did at Sinai.

Jesus told them ahead of time what He was going to do for them. Essentially, He brought His firstfruits offering, the Holy Spirit, and gave it to the church. The timing was perfect, fulfilling the types shown in the feast of Pentecost.

It is interesting that there is the ten-day period between Jesus' ascension and the day of Pentecost. Ten is the number of testing. We all have our faith tested before God bestows the Holy Spirit upon us. The early disciples heeded the word of Jesus and met together to seek God until the Holy Spirit was poured out. They did not know how long it would take. By the ninth day, they may have been getting faint; perhaps some were about ready to give up. People were coming from all over the world to celebrate the Jewish feast the next day. Some wanted to go out and join the celebration. But they persisted in prayer. They did not know from scripture that the Holy Spirit would be poured out on the day of Pentecost. Those reasons were hidden from them. For them, it was a test.

The giving of the law was not tied to the Feast of Pentecost until after the Holy Spirit was given on that day. Many times God keeps things hidden until after their fulfillment. In Moses' day, God wrote the law on tablets of stone. At Pentecost, with the gift of the Holy Spirit, God wrote the law on the disciples' hearts; it was no longer imposed from the outside. With the Holy Spirit living in us, we keep the law from the heart as we live by the Spirit.

The Holy Spirit came upon them suddenly (Acts 2:2).

Flames of fire came to rest on each of them and they began to speak in languages unknown to them. They began to bear witness of the acts of God to all the people of the world who just happened to be in Jerusalem to celebrate the feast.

Notice first that it was sudden. After ten days of nothing but travail after God, He answered all at once. We also need to realize that God gives us a time of testing before He moves us into something new. The testing time is also a time of preparation. The day came at the appointed time, Pentecost, but the disciples did not know that ahead of time. For us, there is also an appointed time. It will come and not delay. But we do not know ahead what that time is. We do need to ready ourselves with fasting and prayer and seeking His face. We are moving into the season of the appointed time. Let us seek His face all the more as we approach the day of fulfillment.

Notice also that types given in the Old Testament for the feast of weeks were fulfilled at Pentecost. This was what all that celebration over the centuries was leading up to: the firstfruits of the Spirit poured out on the church. This was immediately followed by the church witnessing to people from all over the world.

The sending of the Holy Spirit to live in the believers makes Christianity different from all religions. After Jesus rose, He sent the Holy Spirit. Until the Holy Spirit was sent, the church was weak and on the verge of disappearing. With the Holy Spirit, it became strong and grew greatly and swiftly.

The giving of the Spirit did not stop at Pentecost. He has been poured out on believers throughout history from that point onward. The true church of Jesus is always the one living in the power of the Holy Spirit.

We need the Holy Spirit living within us. He is the one who gives us power to live the Christian life. Our own efforts are

FAITH AND PENTECOST

fruitless. We cannot live the Christian life in our own strength. Because He lives within, we can truly live, by living our lives in Him. Let us purpose to live under His direction and not in our own strength. Let us make sure that the Spirit resides within and that He is given control of our lives. Let us renew ourselves in Him daily.

Prayer:

Father, thank You for sending the Holy Spirit. Help me to live by His power every day. I pray in Jesus' name. Amen.

Week 65

Faith and Private Thoughts

For reading and meditation – Acts 10:9-13

"Peter went up on the roof to pray." (v.9)

There are both positive and negative rooftop experiences recorded in the Bible. The spies in Jericho were hidden on the roof (Joshua 2). Samson brought down the roof onto 3000 Philistines (Judges 16). Samuel first met with the future King Saul on the roof (1 Samuel 9:25). David gave in to temptation with Bathsheba while he was on the roof (2 Samuel 11:2). Nebuchadnezzar was on the roof boasting when he was struck dumb for seven years (Daniel 4:29). The paralyzed man was let down through the roof to get close to Jesus (Mark 2:4). Peter was praying on the roof when he had the vision of the unclean animals coming down from heaven (Acts 10).

Roofs in Middle Eastern architecture were flat. A Middle Eastern roof is analogous to a western patio. It is the place where one could relax in private. When we are in private, relaxing, we expose our true hearts. In the above examples, we see

FAITH AND PRIVATE THOUGHTS

a whole spectrum of thought activity from sinful to righteous. What do you think about when relaxing in private?

Whenever we expose our true heart, we find mixture. James 3:10 says, *"Out of the same mouth come praise and cursing. My brothers, this should not be."* David was a man after God's own heart. And yet when he was alone at home, he let his mind and heart drift away to what was sinful. What do we do in private?

There is a part of us that is always private. Our heart or inner intentions and thoughts are always private, except when we let them out. It is in private that we are more likely to let them out. Jesus says to go into your closet to pray (Matthew 6:6). This is in order that your prayer is from your true heart, and so that you will not feed spiritual pride by making others think you are a great pray-er.

There is a problem: we can let out what seems to be righteous from a corrupt heart. We can control, to some degree, what comes out. We can deceive all the people some of the time, and some of the people all of the time, but we cannot deceive all the people all the time, and we can never deceive God.

God always looks on the heart. There is no deceiving Him. He knows our hearts. He sees us on our patio and in our closet.

If God is listening to our hearts, we should, too. Romans 8:13 says, *"For if you live according to the sinful nature, you will die; but if by the Spirit you put to death the misdeeds of the body, you will live."* The only way we can put to death the sinful nature and its deeds is by the Spirit. We must live in the Spirit as much of the time as possible. When temptations arise, or when our minds wander to sinful thoughts, we need to stop what we are doing and call on the Lord for help. We need to fill our minds with His thoughts. We need put our sinful thoughts to death.

Adults usually can control their actions quite well. Because of that, they can live together in community. But controlling their actions does not mean controlling their evil thoughts. Evil people find some way to live out their burning evil passions. It is only by the power of the Holy Spirit that they can be truly set free.

We cannot cure our own heart. We cannot even truly understand our own heart. Jeremiah 17:9 says, *"The heart is deceitful above all things and beyond cure. Who can understand it?"* The heart we were born with is desperately wicked and deceitful. It even lies to us. There is no hope for it except in Jesus. Jesus had a pure heart. He was totally righteous on the inside, the same place where we were totally unrighteous. He gave Himself up so that we could have His righteousness. It is by faith that we appropriate His righteousness. Even though we are fully righteous in God's eyes because He sees Jesus when He looks at us, our inner life must be continually transformed by the power of the Holy Spirit.

When we are on our roof, in our private place, let us examine our hearts to see if we are continually putting to death the things of the flesh by the Holy Spirit. Let us allow the Spirit to transform us from the inside out.

Prayer

Father, help me to continually put to death all those things in me that oppose You. I pray in Jesus' name. Amen.

Week 66

Faith and Storms

For reading and meditation – Acts 27:13-44

"In this way everyone reached land in safety." (v.44)

When Paul was persevering in God's plan for his life, he encountered resistance. He had more storms in his life than anyone I know. Paul exhorted the disciples, *"We must go through many hardships to enter the kingdom of God"* (Acts 14:22). The storms in life will surely come. We will all have many trials. We are expected to pass successfully through all those difficult circumstances. Those storms will strengthen us in the faith. James 1:3-4 says, *"The testing of your faith develops perseverance. Perseverance must finish its work so that you may be mature and complete, not lacking anything."*

Since storms are surely coming, here are some principles to help you navigate your way through them. **First**, prepare for the storms before they come. Jesus says, *"Therefore everyone who hears these words of mine and puts them into practice is like a wise man who built his house on the rock. The rain came down,* *the streams rose, and the winds blew and beat against that house; yet it did not fall, because it had its foundation on the rock"* (Matthew 7:24-25). We prepare for spiritual storms by learning and obeying the word of the Lord. What Jesus says, put into practice. Do not just read the Bible. Do not just listen to sermons. Build your life on those foundations. A strong foundation will help your natural house stand in a flood. A strong foundation in Christian principles will help your life stand in a spiritual flood. Your house keeps out the cold, the wind, the rain and is a comfortable place to live even during the storms. So as we press in to know the Lord and His ways, and to obey Him, we are preparing for storms. We are building protection.

The **second** principle is to stay calm when a storm hits. Jesus was asleep in the boat in the midst of the storm. Mark 4:37-38 says, *"A furious squall came up, and the waves broke over the boat, so that it was nearly swamped. Jesus was in the stern, sleeping on a cushion. The disciples woke him and said to him, 'Teacher, don't you care if we drown?'"* There is a contrast here between Jesus and His disciples. He is calm. They are panicked. Jesus never did anything on earth that He did not expect His disciples to be able to do. If we are prepared for the storm, we will not panic. We will hold our course and navigate safely through, even if it requires a miracle. On the other hand, most of us still have some major shortcomings. There are times we will panic. When that happened to the disciples, they did the right thing. They called out to Jesus to save them. We can do the same.

The **third** principle is to maintain your course during the storm. If you were a pilot and flew into a thunderstorm, the shortest way out would be to fly straight through. Turning around would most likely keep you in the storm for a longer time. It is not a good idea to change your life by making major decisions while you are in the middle of a storm.

FAITH AND STORMS

There will be pressure put on you to change course when the storm hits. Hebrews 12:13 says, *"make straight paths for your feet"* (KJV). When you are in a storm, you need to resist the enemy. Set your sails to adjust to the adverse wind. A sailboat can sail to its destination no matter what direction the wind is blowing. So when that adverse wind comes up, you may have to reset the sail, but maintain the course for the same destination. An interesting note about sailboats is that they only make progress if there is wind blowing. In like manner, we may only make progress spiritually if we are experiencing some trying circumstance.

Sometimes the storm gets out of hand, as it did with the apostle Paul (Acts 27). In this case, the crew did just about everything wrong. They abandoned their course. They even threw away their ability to steer. They abandoned their cargo and they abandoned their hope. This is a lesson in what not to do during a storm. Even with all this despair, God, in His mercy, saved them. We can completely err in our actions during a storm and still be saved, as were the men on the ship. But would it not be better to maintain course and successfully make it through all the storms of life? That is our calling! Let us prepare by growing in our faith. Let us not panic when trials hit, for they surely will. Let us cry out to God when we seem overwhelmed. And let us maintain our course to our destination, so that we can hear the words at the judgment, *"Well done, good and faithful servant!"* (Matthew 25:21).

Prayer

Father, I pray that You would help me prepare for the storms in life, that I may pass through successfully, learning the lessons of life well. I pray in Jesus' name. Amen.

------ Week 67 ------

Faith and the Narrow Way

For reading and meditation – Matthew 7:13-14

"Small is the gate and narrow the road that leads to life, and only a few find it." (v.14)

The walk of faith is a narrow one. There is a deep ditch on each side of the road. If we fail in navigating the road, we end up in the ditch. In attempting to avoid the ditch on one side of the road, we can oversteer, and end up in the ditch on the other side.

We humans are morally weak! If we do not sin deliberately, evil just pops out of our mouth. Temptation is put within our grasp, and we rationalize: "just this once," or "only a little." We may actually successfully navigate past the temptation, only to boast about it. Or we begin by sheer willpower to operate in the flesh instead of the Spirit like the foolish Galatians (see Galatians 3).

The important thing is that we do not stay in the ditch, but get back up on the road. One of the reasons David was called a man after God's own heart is that he was quick to repent and get back in fellowship with God. We will fall from time to time. What do we do about it when we fall? Do we stay down too long? Do we overcompensate, ending up in the ditch on the other side of the road?

We stay in the ditch by not taking corrective action when we sin. We enjoy the season of our sin, thus wandering further from the truth, and making it all the harder to return. We need to be very quick to repent and resume walking on the road. We need to recognize our sin right away and deal with it. God's promise is true: *"If we confess our sins, he is faithful and just and will forgive us our sins and purify us from all unrighteousness"* (1 John 1:9).

Some people think that God is tired of hearing the same confession for the same sin over and over. What Jesus has to say to that is found in Matthew 18:21-22: *"Then Peter came to Jesus and asked, 'LORD, how many times shall I forgive my brother when he sins against me? Up to seven times?' Jesus answered, 'I tell you, not seven times, but seventy-seven times.'"* By this, Jesus is saying that we should do what He does, forgive others every time they sin against us. God will forgive you every time you come to Him in confession and repentance, sincerely from the heart, with intent of never repeating the offense.

Another thing that keeps us from coming straight to God is that we think that the sin is too vile for God to forgive without us doing some penance first. After we have beat on ourselves for a while, we think that we can then go to God and get fixed. This could have serious consequences. Judas betrayed Jesus. He then seemed to do things that showed repentance, but he also killed himself, the ultimate in beating on himself.

The sins on the other side of the road are more subtle. We turn the Christian walk into a list of rules. Do not do this, or do that. We end up living under the law. Paul says, *"You foolish Galatians! Who has bewitched you? Before your very eyes Jesus Christ was clearly portrayed as crucified. I would like to learn just one thing from you: Did you receive the Spirit by observing the law, or by believing what you heard? Are you so foolish? After beginning with the Spirit, are you now trying to attain your goal by human effort?"* (Galatians 3:1-3) We can be so busy doing things for God that we forget to listen to Him. We can lose our joy and our fruitfulness just by doing religious activities. It is crucial to tune in to the Spirit of God, to hear Him, to read scripture, and to walk by the Spirit. If we walk in the flesh, there is no difference between us and anyone else in our society.

We go from one ditch to the other by trying to do away with our sin by our own efforts and will power. It will not work. Only Jesus can deliver us. Remember that Jesus was tempted in every area, yet without sin. If we walk in the Spirit as He did, we also will not fall to temptation. He is changing us into His likeness, so the time will come when we are delivered.

Remember to always go straight to God when you sin. Confess and repent. It does not matter how bad or how often it has happened. God wants you back, and is waiting for your confession and heart repentance. Do not believe the lies that your sin is somehow too bad or that you have to do some kind of penance or that you must overcome it on your own. He will change you as you spend time in fellowship with Him.

Prayer

Father, help me to stay on Your road. When I fall, help me to call out to You quickly in repentance. I pray in Jesus' name. Amen.

Week 68

Faith and Trouble

For reading and meditation – John 15:18-25

"If they persecuted me, they will persecute you also." (v.20)

Jesus came to save us from our sin. He did not come to save us from trouble. If anything, trouble will increase when you become a Christian. The Christian life is the most difficult of all to live. It is the narrow way, not the broad road. You must die to self, not indulge self. Jesus said, *"Whoever finds his life will lose it, and whoever loses his life for my sake will find it"* (Matthew 10:39). Before coming to Christ, we were living for ourselves. Selfishness appears when one is still a small baby. It is the main root of the sin in our lives. Jesus calls us to die to self when we come to Him, and to lose ourselves in Him. Then we will find true life.

It is hard to give up our stuff, our dreams, our choices, our life. We will not do it unless we find a cause bigger than we are. Even after we decide to abandon self for Christ, we find our heart does not change by itself. We may be able to give up the stuff, but we find that we still want it. We can only die, and it is a slow death. Ask the Lord to help you die to self more quickly.

It is not all bad news. Matthew 6:21 says, *"For where your treasure is, there your heart will be also."* If we make choices toward God and His kingdom, we are putting our treasure there. Our treasure consists of more than our physical wealth. It is also our time, our energy, our choices, and our relationships. As we make the right choices toward God, our heart will follow. If we make the right choice of dying to self and living for Jesus, our heart will come along, and we will become less selfish and more Christ-like.

All these choices require faith. Faith will always be tested before it brings forth fruit. All that we do in the Christian faith brings trouble. It is more troublesome to have to believe for something than to just see it and go after it. It is more troublesome to have to wait for the promise until God decides the time is right. Many of Jesus' disciples turned away. Many of His disciples still turn away from Him. They are looking for salvation from their troubles rather than from their sins.

We have troubles because we are being stretched to become more like Jesus. Another type of trouble for all Christians comes from people who oppose Christ. Jesus said, *"If the world hates you, keep in mind that it hated me first"* (John 15:18). If you become a Christian, you cease to belong to the world. Jesus sets us apart from the world. Consequently, the world hates us. It hated Him without a cause. It will hate us without a cause. If we choose to live godly lives, we will suffer persecution for it. It does not matter where we live. Do people persecute you, even in some subtle manner? If not, check yourself. Are you living for God?

The fact that all of nature is in a fallen state is a condition that leads to trouble for us. You will see the sin all around you. When you get a new heart and a transformed mind by becoming a Christian, the world does not change. It is still there in all its filthiness. You are just no longer a part of it. One of the beatitudes will become yours. Matthew 5:4 says, *"Blessed are those who mourn, for they will be comforted."* You will start mourning for the sin of the world that is all around. That is also troubling.

We will have trouble in this world. The good news is that the kingdom of God is breaking into this world. Our sins are gone. We are becoming more like Jesus. Some day there will be no more trouble, but today we need to welcome it, and overcome it, by dying to ourselves and living for Christ. You will be glad you persevered in faith and patience to inherit the promises. (See Hebrews 6:12) It is not easy, but it is going to be worth it!

Prayer

Father, thank You for Your life in me. Help me to choose Your way every time, regardless of the trouble it will bring. I pray in Jesus' name. Amen.

Week 69

Faith and Spiritual Intensity

For reading and meditation – Matthew 11:7-19

"From the days of John the Baptist until now, the kingdom of heaven has been forcefully advancing, and forceful men lay hold of it" (v.12). Or *"the kingdom of heaven suffereth violence, and the violent take it by force"* (KJV).

"Violent" in the above verse means: with energy, forceful, or spiritually intense. It is the spiritually intense who are laying hold of the kingdom of heaven and advancing it. It is the spiritually intense who are waging war on the enemy of our souls and overcoming. We need to become more spiritually intense if we want to be a part of what God is doing in our time, if we want to make a difference in this world.

Spiritual intensity comes from inside us. God stirs us up to seek Him, to focus on Him, to abandon ourselves to Him. We need to respond to Him with our whole heart, our whole selves. This response needs to be a life commitment, not just a couple hours on Sunday morning.

FAITH AND SPIRITUAL INTENSITY

The reason the cloud of God's glory has moved from America to other parts of the world is that the spiritual intensity in the other parts of the world is higher. In America we sit around saying, "God, do something; start a revival, revive my church, my city, my state, my country." There is nothing wrong with praying this way. But then we just sit around and wonder why He does not seem to be doing it.

There is a very good reason why it is not happening. We are God's hands and feet. We are His mouthpiece. He does not do anything on earth without involving His people. He wants us to do it. We need to get out of our comfort zones and take the gospel to our friends and neighbors, to our acquaintances, and to strangers. That is action along with our praying. It is intentionally spreading the good news to our world. However, it cannot be done in our own strength. That is not spiritual intensity.

The spiritually intense do not stop being that way when the worship service is over. They do not stop being that way when they get to work in the morning. They do not ever stop being that way. Their focus is always a spiritual one. The Lord is constantly in their inner thoughts and conversation. They are in continual communion with God. As they communicate with anyone or do any task, one part of their being is focused on the Father and His will for them.

May we all become spiritually intense! I am not there yet. We cannot work up spiritual intensity on our own. Flesh is flesh, no matter how energetic it is. We need to ask God to help us enter that more intense spiritual level.

God wants us more spiritually intense, and He has a plan to get us that way. His plan most likely involves gradual growth as well as big sudden changes. With the slow kind of growth, it may take a while before we notice a change.

LIVING BY FAITH

There are some things that you can definitely do. Spend more time in His presence in prayer and praise. Spend more time in Bible reading and Bible study. Just get to know Him and His ways. Jesus was spiritually intense. He would go out and pray all night. He would welcome interruptions that happened in life as divine appointments to do God's will. He was always focused on His Father's will in every situation.

It is our job to grow as close to the Father as possible. God can use people for eternal ministry more effectively if they are spending lots of quality time with Him. If we spend our time growing close to Him, He will line up divine appointments for us. We will make a difference. We will start taking the kingdom by force. We will become violent in a good way. The devil will be forced to step aside when we come and take back his ground.

Do everything in your power to become spiritually intense. You will find that it is worth it. You will find fulfillment in your calling.

Prayer

Father, I recognize my shortcomings in the area of intensity. Please help me stir up my hunger for You. I pray in Jesus' name. Amen.

Week 70

Faith and Doing It Over

For reading and meditation – Matthew 7:24-27

"But everyone who hears these words of mine and does not put them into practice is like a foolish man who built his house on sand." (v.26)

The children of Israel in the wilderness kept getting the same tests over and over. What should have taken just a few short days of travel to the Promised Land ended up taking forty years because they would not believe. God gave them great promises. He gave them miraculous food every day, shoes that did not wear out, a cloud by day for shelter from the desert sun, and a pillar of fire by night to keep warm in the desert cold. God took care of His people, but they never got to the Promised Land because they complained instead of believing. They kept coming to the same place over and over and not pressing through.

One day, I was redoing the vinyl on a bathroom floor. I made some mistakes in the process, but decided to live with them. The next day, I moved a heavy piece of furniture back into the bathroom. When I slid it on the floor, it ruined the floor right where I had made a mistake. I had not gotten the foundation right. I made a basic mistake in my application of the glue. I did not have help lifting the heavy furniture into place. The result was disaster.

After pulling myself together for a few minutes, I decided I had to redo it. Fixing the mistake proved to be much harder than the extra work to do it right in the first place. The second time around, there were no cut corners, no cheap materials, and no errors. I did it right.

In our Christian walk, we have times that are similar to my experience with the bathroom floor. We have to get our Christian foundations right. What if it is mostly right? I was ready to live with that floor. However, the mistakes and imperfections in the foundation came back to destroy the finished product, so that I had to do it over. In like manner, when our foundational beliefs are off-center, they may appear adequate, but they will not stand the tests of faith that are coming. All that can be shaken will be shaken. In order for us to stand through the testing, the underlying principles of the Bible need to be solidly in place in our lives and in our hearts. If we have covered over or glossed over areas of our lives that are not right, I can see a gash coming to the vinyl of our lives.

God wants to be taken at His word. He said He would give the Promised Land to the people of Israel. Why was it called the Promised Land? All the people had to do was believe enough to go up and take it. They sent twelve spies to go spy it out. Ten of the twelve said that they were not strong enough to take it. They gave an evil report. The people believed them instead of Joshua and Caleb, who said that they were well able to go possess the land. All they had to do was believe. That is all we have to do, too. If we just take God at His word, and believe

FAITH AND DOING IT OVER

in our hearts what He says, we will build a good foundation.

It was God's mercy that the floor tore. I would not have redone it otherwise, and it needed it. In like manner, it is a mercy when we go through really difficult times and have to relearn things. In the end it is worth it to get it right.

When the foundation needs repair, it is never an easy job. There are lots of layers of things covering the foundation. They must be dug through to get to those underlying things on which we base our lives.

When hard circumstances happen, rejoice. God is working towards a more perfect you. Are you willing to be changed into His likeness? Let him do the deep surgery necessary to put your life on the right foundation. Accept joyfully all the circumstances that come your way. His plan for you is to transform you, and sometimes it takes another lap around the mountain.

Prayer

Father, I give You permission to go deep to the foundation in my heart and make it right. I want to be transformed. I pray in Jesus' name. Amen.

Week 71

Three Conditions for Prosperity

For reading and meditation – Psalm 1

"Blessed is the man who does not walk in the counsel of the wicked." (v.1)

There are three conditions that must be present in your life if you want to prosper abundantly. If one of these is missing, you may wonder why things never seem to go right, even though you are accomplishing the other two.

The **first** condition is to **live righteously**. You might say, "I'm a Christian. I have been born again. My sins are forgiven. That makes me righteous, does it not?" As I contemplated this, I asked the Lord, "Is there anything in my life that is unrighteous? Show me, please. I want to live righteously." I did not expect to hear an answer so fast. I was sitting at my computer downloading a program, and up came the one I use for compressing files. The copy I had been using was the evaluation version, good for 10 days. It had been on my computer, unpurchased, for years. I rationalized my lack of purchase since I used the program so infrequently. I was attempting to justify my sin. It was unrighteous. I had a choice: delete the program, or pay for it. I found a free program that does the same thing, so I deleted the compression program and installed its free counterpart. Ask the Lord to show you where you are unrighteous. He will!

Righteousness is a higher standard. It is not just doing enough to get by. It is doing the right thing for the right motive. It is actively resisting temptation. It is getting our hearts right so that our outward actions will be right. *"The righteous cry out, and the L*ORD *hears them; he delivers them from all their troubles"* (Psalm 34:17).

The **second** condition is to return God's **tithe** back to Him. Malachi 3:10 says, *"'Bring the whole tithe into the storehouse, that there may be food in my house. Test me in this,' says the L*ORD *Almighty, 'and see if I will not throw open the floodgates of heaven and pour out so much blessing that you will not have room enough for it.'"* This blessing is for the righteous. It is not for sinners. If an unsaved person tithes, God sees it and honors it. But the first thing He does is draw the unsaved to Himself. Take, for example, the centurion in Caesarea. When Peter arrived, one of the first things he said was that God saw Cornelius' acts of charity. Our tithe, a tenth of our income, is returned to the Lord. We do not pay it, we return it. The tithe is holy unto the Lord. If it is withheld, it is cursed. If it is withheld, there will not be enough. There will always be something that comes up to rob you, so there will not be quite enough. It is because it is cursed if it is not given. It becomes waste. On the other hand, if the tithe is given, it is blessed. The blessing will be great.

I began tithing when I first began earning money on my own. I delivered newspapers starting at age twelve. I had heard about tithing in Sunday school, and began doing it from the start. That was seven years before I was saved. God's first order was not to pour out financial blessing on me. It was to get me saved.

The **third** condition is to **invest in His kingdom**. When one of my children asks me for money, my first response is to ask, "What do you want it for?" If I approve of the project, then the money, if there is any, will be forthcoming. If I disapprove, it will be much harder to get any money out of me. We need to prove to God that our money is going to be used to forward His kingdom. God is not ready to pour out finances on us if we are only motivated to spend them on ourselves.

The law of sowing and reaping comes into effect when we invest in God's kingdom. You need to sow seeds. There is no harvest without a planting. Where are you sowing seeds? This sowing of seeds is over and above living righteously and tithing.

If you want a harvest of souls, then sow seeds of the gospel. If you want to participate in the harvest of a ministry, then sow seeds into that ministry by giving to it. If you want to prosper, sow seeds to the poor, helping them to prosper. Crops come back in kind. If you sow tomato seeds, you get tomatoes. You get the same kind that you sow. You get it later than you sow it, and you get more of it than you sow. Do not destroy your harvest by not tithing and not living righteously. All three are necessary: living righteously, tithing, and sowing seeds. Do these things and your world will change. God promises it.

Prayer

Father, show me an unrighteous area in my life that You want me to clean up. Help me do it. Guide me in how best to invest in expanding your kingdom on earth. Thank You, in Jesus' name. Amen.

---— Week 72 ---—

Faith and Favor

For reading and meditation – Exodus 3

"And I will make the Egyptians favorably disposed toward this people, so that when you leave you will not go empty-handed." (v.21)

God favors His people. If we are living right and loving the Lord with all our hearts, then we can expect God's favor. An example of favor is receiving a great deal without even asking for it.

I was interested in purchasing some carpet to install in an apartment that I rent out. The store was having a sale, and I was quoted a price that was 20 percent off the listed price. I thought about it overnight, and then returned to complete the purchase. I gave them the quote to make sure I got the lower price. They looked it up and sold the carpet to me for an additional discount. The salesman said, "It looks like this is your lucky day." The carpet was ordered and I arranged to pick it up when it arrived. When I arrived at the store to pick up the carpet, after calling and arranging to rent their truck, I found that the truck was out and would be unavailable for several hours. Consequently, I went home, discouraged. Two days later, they delivered the carpet free of charge. That is favor. In this case, my patience was tried before the favor was granted.

This type of provision should be happening for us all the time. In the early church, everyone was living under favor because of the generosity of all the saints. Acts 2:45 says, *"Selling their possessions and goods, they gave to anyone as he had need."* Luke 6:38 says, *"Give, and it will be given to you. A good measure, pressed down, shaken together and running over, will be poured into your lap. For with the measure you use, it will be measured to you."*

You determine the level of favor that God gives you. It is measured to you according to the measure you use. If you are tight with your giving, then you can expect the same measure of favor. Are you generous with your gifts? Then you can expect generous favor. It will not necessarily come from where you give it. Because you have given it in Jesus' name for the furtherance of the kingdom, He keeps track of it. He is the one who ordains favor for you. It can and does come from anywhere and usually unexpectedly, without asking.

Your giving is not only financial, but also time and talents. However you give, it will be measured back to you. Remember the law of sowing and reaping. Giving is sowing. Do you sow bountifully or sparingly? When there is less money, do you give anyway? Do you give a higher or lower percentage than regular when you receive a bonus or a windfall? Do you want to receive God's favor?

It felt really good when I received God's favor with the free delivery of that carpet. It was so obvious to me that God's hand was in it. It reassured me that He loves me and cares for me. We do not need to continually think about sowing and reaping, but just act in obedience, and do our part in blessing others and bringing them into the kingdom. The blessings we receive are little assurances from God that we are doing the right thing, and that our Father loves us.

The great thing is that God <u>wants</u> to bless us. It is His delight to do good to His children. However, God has limited Himself by accountability to the scriptures. They explain how He blesses His people. It is in proportion to the measure they use to give. God is bound by that. He wants to bless you, but can only do so to the degree that you give of what you have. So loosen your hand. Give a little more. Be generous with your time, your service, your talents. By doing so, you unbind the hands of God to bless you. Then give thanks when the favor comes!

Prayer

Father, thank You for Your favor. Help me to be more generous with my time, talent, and resources. I pray in Jesus' name. Amen.

Week 73

Faith and Focus

For reading and meditation – Matthew 22:34-40

"Love the LORD your God with all your heart and with all your soul and with all your mind. This is the first and greatest commandment." (vs.37-38)

We need to love God first. We need to seek His kingdom first. Jesus said, *"But seek first his kingdom and his righteousness, and all these things will be given to you as well"* (Matthew 6:33). We should put Him first with all we have, with all our heart, our mind, and our soul. This is focus. Focus is concentration of attention. His kingdom and righteousness are to be our primary life focus. We should concentrate our life energy on loving God, seeking His kingdom, and living in His righteousness.

Jesus' absolute focus for His life was to please His Father. He only did what He saw the Father doing. He lived out the Father's plan for His life perfectly. Those of us with a sin problem (that is, the rest of us), are always falling short, but that should not stop us. God describes David as one, *"who kept my*

FAITH AND FOCUS

commands and followed me with all his heart, doing only what was right in my eyes" (1 Kings 14:8). We all know that David fell short in many ways. But God forgave and forgot all of that. He only saw David's righteous and repentant heart. He only saw David's focus on what was right. In the same way, when we repent from our various sins, God no longer holds them against us. He no longer remembers them. He remembers our righteousness. He remembers our proper focus.

How do we focus on God? We cannot see Him except by faith. We cannot hear Him except by faith. It is through the eyes and ears of faith that we approach God. We believe the Bible by faith. We receive the Holy Spirit by faith. We walk the Christian life by faith. We focus on our relationship with God by faith.

Even those saints who have the most insight receive their revelation by faith. This is a faith walk. God honors our faith, and calls us righteous.

The difference between the Pharisees and Abraham is one that we need to examine. God honored Abraham, but condemned the Pharisees. Why? Abraham had a relationship with God. He had conversations with God that were recorded in the Bible. Abraham focused on God. He put God first. Of course, he had many shortcomings, just like everyone else, but when God looked at Abraham's heart, it was trusting, repentant, and obedient.

What about the Pharisees? What they taught, they had no intention of doing themselves. It was all appearance, but no heart. Jesus condemns them not for what they do, but for what they do not do. What they did not do was believe from the heart. It was all for show. I am sure that was not true of all the Pharisees, but it seemed to be the general rule.

We need to be honest with ourselves. Are we hiding sin in

our heart? Or, are we confessing and repenting to God? Do we believe in our heart? Or, do we just have a lot of head knowledge? If we believe in our heart, we will act on that belief. We will trust God like we trust the law of gravity. Do we keep our focus on God, or at least refocus on Him, on a regular daily basis? Do we take inventory of our lives, clearing up anything that hinders our relationship to God?

Remember, it is the first and greatest commandment to love God with all your heart, with all your soul, with all your mind. This needs to be first in our heart every day. We all fall short, but we can all improve. Live not for appearances, but from your heart, wholly for God.

Prayer

Father, help me to focus my whole heart on You and live every day from a love relationship with You. I pray in Jesus' name. Amen.

Week 74

Faith and Deliverance

For reading and meditation – Psalm 34

"A righteous man may have many troubles, but the Lord delivers him from them all." (v.19)

What does it mean to be righteous? Too often we look at ourselves, citing our sins and saying, "I guess this promise is not for me, since I know that I sin." But we need to look at righteousness from God's perspective. We are in Christ. When the Father looks at us, He sees Jesus. Jesus did not sin. Jesus took our sin at the cross. We are perfect in Him. We are righteous from the Father's perspective. We qualify as righteous if we are in Christ. God gives us His righteousness.

Our righteousness qualifies us for deliverance from trouble. What exactly does that mean? It cannot mean that we will not have troubles, because the verse itself says, *"A righteous man may have many troubles."* I looked up the word for "delivers" in the Hebrew, and there is a whole range of meaning, from removing the trouble from us, to giving us grace to go through it. Basically, it means that troubles will not overcome us. The Lord allows our troubles, and uses them to make us more like Jesus. His focus is not on our living a trouble-free life. That kind of life would cause us to become lukewarm. In the midst of trouble, we grow in our faith, and are motivated to have fervor for God.

Our faith needs to be solid in the fact that all troubles will end. God will deliver us from our troubles. The devil will not be allowed to win the contest against the righteous. Remember Job. He endured extreme trials. It took a long time, but in the end, he was doubly blessed.

There are lots of people going through the most major trouble of their lives right now. But we can be sure that the righteous will come through their troubles, and that they will end up better people for it. That is God's plan for troubles. They are to backfire on the devil, and to help the righteous draw nearer to Jesus. The great trials in our nations will also cause many people to come to Jesus for the first time, and others to come back to Him after having departed from His ways. There will be much fruit. The devil's plan to destroy our countries will completely backfire.

What do we do about troubles? First, we believe that God has a purpose in them to draw us closer to Him. Second, we believe that they are temporary. Third, we believe God for His deliverance.

God is the one who controls your circumstances. He will resolve the trouble, or deliver you, or whatever is needed, at just the right time. He knows you. He knows how much you can take. He believes you can go through any trial that He allows to come your way. He makes sure that your trials are not harder than you can endure. He knows just when to say, "Enough!"

With each trial is the grace to go through it. We may see

FAITH AND DELIVERANCE

some Christians going through trials that we think would be too hard for us. But remember, He gives us His grace when we need it. If we are not having a particular trial, we do not need the grace for it at that moment.

What does this assurance mean? It means we can volunteer for the hardest, riskiest duty as believers. It means we can take chances. It means we can survive disaster. And even if we die, we still make it through the trouble by landing in the arms of the Savior.

The Christian life should be the most exciting of lives. Who else has the faith to go through anything? So go for it. Take risk. Trust God for all your circumstances. Do not hold back in fear; volunteer! Live an exciting rather than a safe life. You will have troubles, but you also will be delivered from them. You will grow and be blessed by going through these troubles and becoming an overcomer.

Prayer

Father, help me to be more bold for You, knowing that You will bring me through every trial. I pray in Jesus' name. Amen.

Week 75

Faith, Listening and Looking

For reading and meditation – John 3:1-8

"I tell you the truth, no one can see the kingdom of God unless he is born again." (v.3)

Those who have been born again can see the kingdom of God. We have heard the message, and have received faith. We can see, but do we look? We can hear, but do we listen? We have a serious problem. We do most of our looking with our eyes. We do most of our hearing with our ears. Those two organs work well if we are observing things of this world. But for us who have been born again, it is not this world that we need to look into and listen for, it is the kingdom of God.

We need to develop seeing with the eyes of our heart and hearing with the ears of our heart. This is how we develop faith. Jesus speaks to us not just during our quiet times, not just during church services. He speaks to us constantly. Do we ever stop to listen? He is speaking to you right now, and it is not just the words on this page.

FAITH, LISTENING AND LOOKING

How do I know His voice? There is so much clatter of voices. There is the voice of the tempter. Can you recognize him? There is the voice of the world. Can you recognize it? Can you turn it off? Without the clatter of other voices, His voice is easier to recognize and hear. Jesus says, *"My sheep listen to my voice; I know them, and they follow me"* (John 10:27).

You can listen to God's voice; Jesus says so. Tune your ear to hear His voice. The above verse also says, *"they follow me."* Within the meaning of "to listen" is "to obey." Our listening must be followed up with obedience. When we are disobedient to His voice, doubt arises. I have not always obeyed, which grieves the Lord. He speaks more softly and less frequently after that for a while, until I repent. When I do not listen, I am also grieved. Some of us are slower learners than others. Becoming good at obeying His voice will save the pain of grief, and keep us from regressing on the Christian path. We can hear His voice and know when He speaks. It is by faith.

As a believer, you can also see the kingdom of God. Do you actively look for it? Again, the seeing is with your heart. It is within you. If we start looking for God's kingdom, we will see it. We will see it all around. Not by looking with our eyes, but by looking with faith in our hearts.

To see the kingdom, we need to see things the way God sees them. He loves everyone, and sees the full potential for which each of us was created. Jesus died for sinners before they were converted. He loved them and saw their possibilities. We need to begin seeing people that way.

If we see the kingdom, and hear God's voice on a regular basis, then our behavior will start to change. We will become more optimistic. We will see the many victories of God in this world and rejoice. We will see all the ways He cares for each of us, and thank Him. We will start to see the potential in others and encourage them in faith towards their destiny in Christ. We will encourage them to become hearers and seers, too.

Our blinders are our sins. They stand in the way of our seeing. We need to cry out for mercy and receive forgiveness and changed hearts. The blinders will fall off. We will begin to see and hear and participate in the kingdom.

Start listening to His voice. He is speaking. Obey what you hear. Start looking for His kingdom. You can see it. Keep doing these things, and your faith will grow.

Prayer

Thank you, Father, for speaking to us every day. Help us to hear and obey. We pray in Jesus' name. Amen!

Week 76

God's Purpose in Storms

For reading and meditation – Mark 4:35-41

"Jesus was in the stern, sleeping on a cushion. The disciples woke him and said to him, 'Teacher, don't you care if we drown?'"
(v.38)

Jonah did not want to obey God and go to Ninevah to preach, so he took a boat to Tarshish (Jonah 1:1-4). God sent a great storm that threatened to break up the boat. The sailors were terrified. When they threw Jonah, the offending party, overboard (v.15), the sea grew calm.

In another storm, God speaks to Paul about the storm ahead of time (Acts 27:9-44). Paul, in turn, directs those on board the ship, and all are saved, even though the ship is lost.

In a third storm, Jesus is asleep in the back of the boat when the storm comes up. The disciples are terrified. They awaken Jesus who calms the storm with a word (Mark 4:36-41).

God has different purposes in storms. The first storm had one purpose for Jonah (to get him back on God's path), and another purpose for the ship's crew. It confirmed their faith in the true God, and the need to do right and not sin. Sometimes storms come up in our lives to get us back on the track we deliberately left. Jonah deliberately left God's plan for him. God did not give up on Jonah. He will not give up on you. You might say, "I think I will go my own way for a while, and not Your way for me." It would be His mercy to send you a storm. Pray that He will, when you deliberately get off track. You are special to God. He will never give up on you. His storms are also His mercies. He will make things very uncomfortable for you, so you will not enjoy your continuance in sin. He has a plan to get you back on His path. It may not be fun. How can you say that it is fun to spend three days in the belly of a whale? Even though it may be quite painful, you will surely be thankful for it in the end.

If the first storm is to get those back on track who are running from God deliberately, the second storm is for those who are following God with their whole hearts. Paul, God's servant, was wholly committed to doing God's will. He still had a storm to endure. There is a difference here. In Paul's storm and subsequent shipwreck, God let him know what was to happen, how it could be avoided, and how the damage could be lessened. Amos 3:7 says, *"Surely the Sovereign LORD does nothing without revealing his plan to his servants the prophets."*

Today, the Lord is speaking to His prophets also. He is telling them about the storms that are coming to the world and to our country. He also is telling them what to tell His people so that the damage can be minimized. There is nothing new in what the prophets are telling us to do: humble ourselves, pray, seek God's face, turn from our wicked ways (2 Chronicles 7:14). When God's people pray, the damage from storms can be avoided or lessened. If we listen to the prophets when they

GOD'S PURPOSE IN STORMS

tell us how to avert a worse crisis, we are wise. God spoke to Paul, but everyone else had to listen to Paul to know what to do to avoid the crisis.

When they did not heed the advice, the storm still came and the ship was lost. Paul was following God wholeheartedly and still suffered greatly. However, his most precious faith was not damaged. It increased. The same will happen to us if we follow God wholeheartedly. We may not avoid the storm, but our faith and that of those around us will grow.

In the third type of storm, you are not deliberately running from God. You are on His team. You are growing in faith, but certainly not at a point in life where you are ready to be launched. Jesus is there, but He is asleep in your boat. This storm gets your attention. It makes you cry out to Jesus. When He calms the storm, your faith grows. You are totally in awe of Him. You did not hear from God this time like Paul did. You were not running from God this time like Jonah was. Still, you had a storm. You called on Jesus, and He saved you from it. Your faith grew stronger.

There is no way to avoid storms in life. Regardless of where you are in your walk with God, there will be storms. These storms are designed with you in mind, to strengthen you, to test you, to help you get back on track, and to help you grow. You will be a better person when you emerge from the storms God sends your way. So persevere, and make it through them.

Prayer

Father, thank You for the storms You are sending my way. Help me to persevere through them. I pray in Jesus' name. Amen.

Week 77

Faith and Being Sent

For reading and meditation –Matthew 9:35-38

"The harvest is plentiful but the workers are few. Ask the Lord of the harvest, therefore, to send out workers into his harvest field." (vs.37-38)

There has always been a shortage of Christian workers. The task of world evangelization and discipleship is huge. We are to pray that God would send more workers.

Every year, Wycliffe Bible Translators would like to recruit over one hundred school teachers to teach their workers' children. They always come up short. At the same time, the applications for public school teachers in Oregon, where I live, overflow in every school district. Pray for the workers to be sent out.

Who is the person that God sends? We can learn the answer from the following passages.

In Isaiah 6:8 the Lord says, *"Whom shall I send? And who will go for us?"* And Isaiah answers, *"Here am I. Send me!"* In

FAITH AND BEING SENT

John 17:18 Jesus says, *"As you sent me into the world, I have sent them into the world."* In John 20:21-22 Jesus says, *"As the Father has sent me, I am sending you... Receive the Holy Spirit."*

God is looking for volunteers. I used to pray Isaiah's prayer, "Here am I; send me," on a regular basis. God has a plan for winning the world, and I have a desire to be a part of it. If that is your desire, then you also are a candidate to volunteer, to pray Isaiah's prayer. God is actually looking for volunteers. You do not have to wait around for a big calling. If you desire to serve, He takes volunteers. Isaiah volunteered. I volunteered, and He sent me to the Philippines for 15 years.

Even though I am no longer in the Philippines, I am still sent. In John 17, Jesus sends us into the world. We are sent. It is a matter of faith. The more we believe we are sent, the more we will bear fruit in all the circumstances of our lives.

When Jesus sent the disciples, He breathed the Holy Spirit on them. One of the main reasons for receiving the Holy Spirit is to have God's power when we go into the world as sent ones.

When I am given an opportunity to speak or serve in any capacity, I need to remember that it really is God who not only opened up the opportunity, but also sent me. I am sent when God opens opportunity to speak for Him in the supermarket or on the job or with a neighbor or with anyone who happens to cross my path. Since I believe I am sent in those situations, I need to be praying for God to show me how to minister in each circumstance. I can receive an answer, act on it, and believe that God will speak through me.

I heard Dr. T.L. Osborn speak at a conference. He was a missionary to more than ninety countries over the previous fifty-seven years. He said that wherever he goes and whenever he speaks, he believes God sent him. He always tells the people that God sent him, because he believes it.

We can all follow that example. We can believe that God sends us to each person or group that we encounter. We can start believing that God knows how He wants us to minister to each person. We can sense the Holy Spirit prompting us, and hear His still small voice for each encounter that we have.

If we believe that God is sending us, we will have more impact for Him than if we do not. It is by faith that we follow Him. Our faith in believing that He sent us will be honored. I believe He inspired me with this message for you today. Now go, believing that He is sending you, too. Make an impact in your world!

Prayer

Father, help me to believe that my life is a mission for You. Help me to treat each encounter as preordained by You. I pray in Jesus' name. Amen.

Week 78

Faith and Worship

For reading and meditation – John 4:21-26

"A time is coming and has now come when the true worshipers will worship the Father in spirit and truth, for they are the kind of worshipers the Father seeks." (v.23)

What is true worship? I was once in a worship service where very few people seemed to be truly worshiping. While I was lost in worship, the person beside me nudged me and said, "I'm bored."

It is not the music that makes for worship, even though music may help facilitate it. The key is listening to and responding to the Holy Spirit.

The worship God desires has two aspects: spirit and truth. It may be expressed in music or words or actions. There is no set pattern. All the music or words or actions, however, can be done without any worship proceeding to God. The actual worship, although it takes music or words or actions, is not those things. You can go through all the motions, and maybe even convince everyone that you are worshiping God, but it may not be happening.

Worship does not have any specific location. You do not have to go to a church building to worship. In fact, you would be far better off if you worshiped all week, rather than just the few times you are in company with other believers.

Worship has to come from the heart, our hearts in tune with the Holy Spirit. That is worship in spirit. We need to prepare our hearts for worship. We need to examine ourselves to make sure we are not holding on to secret sins. We need to ask forgiveness, and decide to obey God. We need to humble ourselves before Him. Once the channel between us and God is clear, then we can truly worship.

The prerequisite for worship is a clean heart before God. Jesus said, *"If you are offering your gift at the altar and there remember that your brother has something against you, leave your gift there in front of the altar. First go and be reconciled to your brother; then come and offer your gift"* (Matthew 5:23-24). Our hearts must be right before God and man before we can truly worship. Otherwise, we will find ourselves going through all the motions, but finding our hearts far away. Do you examine yourself before each worship time?

Stronger worship will come as a result of stronger radical obedience by faith. God is looking for a higher level of obedience. We may say we want higher and better worship. We may say we want to see God respond to our worship with a visitation of power. Our radical obedience to Him by faith opens the way.

How has your obedience been lately? Abraham obeyed in the face of danger and uncertainty. It certainly did not make much sense to sacrifice his only son, the son of promise. But he did it in radical obedience to God as an act of worship. As

FAITH AND WORSHIP

a result of Abraham's obedience, God said to him, *"I will surely bless you and make your descendants as numerous as the stars in the sky and as the sand on the seashore"* (Genesis 22:17).

If we believe the truth of the scripture, we act on it in faith. That action is the obedience that God is looking for. Radical obedience will always test us. God is good at hard tests. He believes we are ready for the tests that He gives us. When we obey Him with joy, even if it is hard, it is radical obedience. That obedience, in itself, is an act of worship.

When we all decide we are going to live our lives with that kind of obedience, our worship times will come alive. If we worship God, we are saying He is Lord. If He is Lord, we need to obey Him. He is waiting for us to radically obey Him.

Prayer

Father, help me to worship You in spirit and truth. Help me to obey You fully. I ask these things in Jesus' name. Amen.